South Yorkshire Mining Disasters
Volume 2

The Twentieth Century

Rescuer wearing Proto breathing apparatus returning from a disaster. NUM

South Yorkshire Mining Disasters
Volume 2

The Twentieth Century

BRIAN ELLIOTT

MINING HERITAGE SERIES

Series Editor

Brian Elliott

Wharncliffe Books

> **For my father, Fred Elliott,**
> **who worked at Wharncliffe Woodmoor**
> **1, 2 & 3 Colliery**

First published in Great Britain in 2009 by
Wharncliffe Books
an imprint of
Pen & Sword Books Ltd
47 Church Street
Barnsley
South Yorkshire
S70 2AS

Copyright © Brian Elliott 2009

ISBN 978-1-84563-057-7

Typeset in 10pt Palatino by
Mac Style, Beverley, East Yorkshire.

Printed and bound in the UK by
the MPG Books Group

Pen & Sword Books Ltd incorporates the Imprints of Pen & Sword Aviation, Pen & Sword Maritime, Pen & Sword Military, Wharncliffe Local History, Pen and Sword Select, Pen and Sword Military Classics and Leo Cooper.

For a complete list of Pen & Sword titles please contact
PEN & SWORD BOOKS LIMITED
47 Church Street, Barnsley, South Yorkshire, S70 2AS, England
E-mail: enquiries@pen-and-sword.co.uk
Website: www.pen-and-sword.co.uk

Contents

Foreword

In this second volume of his history of mine disasters in South Yorkshire, Brian Elliott has produced an impressive and moving tribute to the thousands of men who died.

From the disaster at Aldwarke Main in 1904, to the tragedy at Bentley in 1978, this history graphically brings to life the perilous working conditions underground. Through meticulous research, Brian has woven into his account of the individual disasters the testimonies of those who were there. Viscerally, we feel what it was like to enter a pit scorched by 'gob fire', or deluged by flood, or one that had been crushed by a catastrophic fall.

Yet it is not only those who died who are commemorated in the pages of this book. Behind each one of these horrific tragedies lie stories of remarkable heroism: the bravery of those who risked their lives to save the victims of disaster shines through. The book is as uplifting as it is harrowing. It is a tribute to that intense, almost mystical bond that existed between the miners, and between their families in the villages above the pits where they worked.

Catherine Bailey
Author of *Black Diamonds*

Surprise Surprise

The placards read

MINING DISASTER
30 DEAD

Mining disasters
Are spaced through the years
Like volcanoes erupting
And snow at Whitsuntide.

Through the years
The same pit-head shots
The quiet groups,
The children largely still.
The manager
In white official's helmet,
Stern faced
Like a headmaster late for morning prayers.

And we're shocked to read
That a few steel props
Can't hold
A billion tons of rock,
That a cutting machine
Can spark a light
Causing undetected gas
To ignite.

And next time
We'll be just as shocked.
We'll pick up the papers and say
You wouldn't think this could happen today.

Barry Hines

From *This Artistic Life* (a new anthology)
published by Pomona Books (2009)
www.pomonauk.co.uk

Introduction

I spent my childhood in the South Yorkshire pit village of Carlton, near Barnsley. The spoil heap of Wharncliffe Woodmoor 1, 2 & 3 colliery dominated the skyline at the bottom of our street. For me and my friends the muckstack was like a great magnet, attracting scores of us to play up and down its black, grey and dangerously-looking red-hot smoking slopes, much to our parents' consternation. Most local families had some connection with the pit and pit-work wasn't so much an occupation as a way of life.

My father was an underground fitter at the colliery, repairing, maintaining and installing machinery. Like most of his mates he had started work straight from school, at the age of fourteen, then progressing through a variety of tasks. It was a skilled job and not without its dangers and mishaps. At times he worked all three shifts, known as days, 'afters' and nights. There were always a few moments of anxiety that my mother clearly felt after she had kissed him goodbye on his way to work. And when he was late home the worry returned. Even as a small but perhaps not too sensitive boy I could not help to feel a little concerned too; and my younger sister felt the same way. Not surprising really. He had narrow escapes and was injured on a number of occasions; and the dreadful August morning in 1936, when an underground explosion resulted in the deaths of 58 men, was still fresh in his memory. Although not working on that night shift, he witnessed the pit-top

Fred Elliott (centre) with Keith Jones (left) and Brian Summerfield, in the pit yard, Wharncliffe Woodmoor 1, 2 & 3 Colliery. Author's collection

scenes, including the transfer of bodies to his old school across from the pit; and Lawrence, his elder brother, helped with the rescue operations.

Although this book is about disasters and serious accidents involving multiple fatalities, it was the day-to-day accidents which were, by far, the most common causes of deaths in mines. In the thirty years after 1880 there was an average of four miners killed and 517 injured every day in British coal mines. Even in 1913, the year of Senghendydd, when 439 men and youths were killed in what remains Britain's worst mine disaster, 656 miners died in everyday accidents. The disasters provided spectacular copy for local and regional newspapers, but coverage was small or non existent when one or two men were involved. Jim McFarlene, in his book *The Blood on Your Coal*, explains this dichotomy very well:

> Day to day loss of life in the pits, the sniping accidents of industrial warfare, killed far more mineworkers than were killed in colliery disasters, yet there was little publicity or public awareness of that fact. Colliery disasters, like great battles, are dramatic events which forced themselves on the public consciousness.

Perhaps the most important point to make and remember is that when an accident or disaster occurs it leaves a legacy rarely forgotten. Again, we can refer to McFarlene's eloquent words: 'This daily carnage of industrial war dug deep into the soul of of the mining communities, leaving social scars which remain long after public interest has faded.' The recent dedication and rededication of mining memorials and special events certainly demonstrate this situation. In Yorkshire, an annual service of remembrance, recently instigated by the NUM, has and will continue to be appreciated by thousands of former miners, their families and friends.

Gradually, and then quite markedly after the nationalisation of the coal mining industry in 1947, safety and working conditions improved. In the twelve years ending 31 December 1867 there were 12,590 people killed in colliery accidents in Great Britain, equivalent to an accident rate of 357 per 100,000 employed. The rate fell to 216 (1214 deaths) in 1885 and reduced to 62 (460 deaths) in 1949. By the early 1970s, mining coal was a far less hazardous occupation than it had been even a generation earlier. But it remained a dangerous job. In 1970–71 there were 92 fatalities in NCB mines at a rate of 30 per 100,000. My cousin, George Eastwood, was one the 1970s statistics, killed at Grimethorpe Colliery, aged 37. Occasional multiple fatality accidents did occur, in Yorkshire most notably at Lofthouse and Houghton Main (where my Uncle, Frank Elliott, worked); and the Bentley man-riding accident in 1978 highlighted an area where the Health and Safety Executive, Mines Inspectorate, NCB management and unions continued to express great concern.

This book concludes more than five years' research on coalmining disasters in the modern county of South Yorkshire, from early times until the late 1970s. Even so, it is not intended as an academic study, nor is it meant to be morbidly inclined; but rather a useful overview of a series of events that really did form the soul of our social and industrial past. Throughout the research and writing I have been conscious, particularly in respect of this volume, of an increasing awareness and interest in family history. Hopefully, the books will provide contexts for anyone with ancestors or recent family members who were involved in colliery disasters.

Strictly speaking a disaster involved ten or more deaths but, as in the first volume, I have included serious multiple fatality accidents below this figure in order to provide a more complete, more human narrative. Several of the larger disasters, such as at Cadeby (1912),

Bentley (1931) and Wharncliffe Woodmoor (1936), and indeed a good number of others, have sufficient research material for extensive studies and individual books. Though space has limited their inclusion here, I do hope their entries do justice to the scale of each event.

Oral testimony from the twentieth century disasters is getting less each year due to the passing of mining veterans, family members and friends. Wherever possible I have tried to make use of this relatively unexplored source. These are the voices of people who were there and are usually not recorded in any other medium. At the same time I have tried to be sensitive during the writing process since so many of the accidents and disasters are of course within living memory. For the last few entries, a later interpretation will be required, for reasons that I have explained when introducing each event.

The book follows the same chronological format as the first volume, and once again I have added a short glossary of relevant mining terms.

Many individuals and organisations have assisted me during the course of the research for this volume. In particular I would like to thank my publishers, Pen & Sword Books, of Barnsley, for commissioning the book and having the patience to wait so long for its completion. Catherine Bailey did not hesitate to my request for her to write a foreword, for which I am immensely thankful. Special thanks too to Barry Hines, Eleanor Hines and Mark Hodkinson of Pomona Books for permission to reproduce *Surprise Surprise*. Once again, I am indebted to the kindness of Ian Winstanley and his Coal Mining History Resource Centre website (now owned by the Barnsley-based solicitors Raleys). Also thanks to Philip Thompson and his colleagues at the National Union of Mineworkers in Barnsley. Mel Dyke was ever supportive as usual; as was Andrew Featherstone. Lord Mason provided access to the House of Lords Library (and his own reminiscences). Geoffrey Howse generously provided accommodation for me when I was undertaking research in London. A fuller list of acknowledgements is set out below and further credits are given in the Sources and Bibliography section. My sincere apologies for any omissions.

People

Catherine Bailey, Bill Bennett, Louisa Bentley, Giles Brearley, John Cooksey and family, Barry Crabtree, Barrie Dalby, Tony Dodsworth, Mel Dyke, Norman Ellis, Andrew Featherstone, Ray Haigh, Lynn Haines, Barry Hines, Eleanor Hines, Geoffrey Howse, Martyn Johnson, Rebecca Lawther, Rt Hon the Lord Mason of Barnsley, Sam Owens, Harry Owens, Chris and Pearl Sharp (Old Barnsley), Alice Rodgers, Francis Thompson, Philip Thompson, Karen Walker, Jon Wilkinson, Paul Wilkinson, Bruce Wilson and Ian Winstanley.

Organisations

Barnsley Chronicle Archives, Barnsley Library (Local Studies & Archives), British Newspaper Library (Colindale), Doncaster Archives, Doncaster & District Family History Society, Doncaster Library (Local Studies), Eyre & Spotiswood Ltd, The Library of the House of Lords, Health & Safety Executive, Lancashire County Library and Information Service, Pen and Sword Books, Pomona Books, National Coal Mining Museum for England, National Union of Mineworkers, Rotherham Library (Local Studies & Archives) and Sheffield Local Studies Library.

Part One

Early Twentieth-Century Disasters
1900–1910

"…our lamps were put out by the vibration, and we lay together in the cage…It was a fearful time. I said my prayers."

George Hargreaves, Barrow cage disaster survivor

Serious winding and shaft accidents were rare in the modern era. Before the First World War the great majority of engines were steam-powered. The introduction of electricity in mining was relatively slow compared with other industries. As late as 1949, two years after

NUM (Yorkshire Area) Barrow Branch banner at the centenary service and commemoration of the 1907 pit cage disaster, Birdwell, near Barnsley, 17 November 1907. The author

nationalisation, little more than 50 per cent of the power used at collieries was electrical. The men who operated the winders were generally experienced and trustworthy, in fact it was a job which was often carried on through several generations. The engines became more efficient and powerful, capable of hauling cages in many deep shafts at great speed. The cages in which men and materials were vertically transported varied considerably from mine to mine. Some had double or even triple decks and, certainly in the early years of the century, were small and cramped where the circumference of old shafts was small, with so-called safety bars offering minimum protection from being spilled out during a sudden mishap. The wire steel winding ropes had long replaced hemp and were supplied by reputable companies. Ropes were routinely inspected for wear and tear on a daily basis and replaced within a sensible 'use by' date. But the potential for technical failure and human error remained ever present. The new century dawned with two major winding incidents resulting in the deaths of fourteen men.

When a cage containing miners hurled uncontrollably to the bottom of the shaft – or jerked suddenly, spilling its travellers – the consequence was of course horrendous carnage, usually with no chance of survival. However, as we shall see, some remarkable escapes from death did occur, as well as acts of great heroism. Exceptionally, two very serious winding accidents took place at separate South Yorkshire pits within a short time-span: at Aldwarke Main, near Rotherham and in the Barnsley area, at Barrow Colliery.

(1) Aldwarke Main

Location: Aldwarke, Rotherham
Type: Winding accident
Fatalities: 7
Date: Tuesday, 23 February 1904

Aldwarke Main was purchased by the well known Sheffield steelmakers John Brown & Company (Limited) in 1873. Browns soon become famous shipbuilders, taking over a Clydebank yard towards the end of the century. At the time of the accident the company had already begun work on the ill-fated liner, HMS *Lusitania* which was to make its maiden voyage in 1907. Aldwarke was the choice part of Brown's Rotherham area coalmining interests, which included Car House and Rotherham Main collieries. The importance of Brown's mining enterprise was reflected in a large workforce of over 4,500 men.

The accident occurred in the No 2 upcast shaft of the Parkgate pit. It was used for man riding and was also an outlet for the steam from the hauling engines. Close by was the No 1 shaft which actually wound the Parkgate coal. Both shafts were eighteen feet in diameter, almost entirely brick-lined, and extended to about 405 yards.

Two early morning 'draws' had already taken place without amiss, each one lowering eight men contained in the double-decker cage to the pit bottom. At 5.20 am, the third draw commenced, but the winding rope snapped about eighty yards from the bottom. The 4–5 ton cage crashed partly through the floor into the sump, its lower part telescoping into the upper section. It's hard to imagine the horror that the miners felt in the few seconds of their final descent, or indeed the shock and fear of their underground friends – and several hundred pit-top colleagues, who had been waiting to follow them.

Aldwarke Main in the early 1900s. Tony Dodsworth

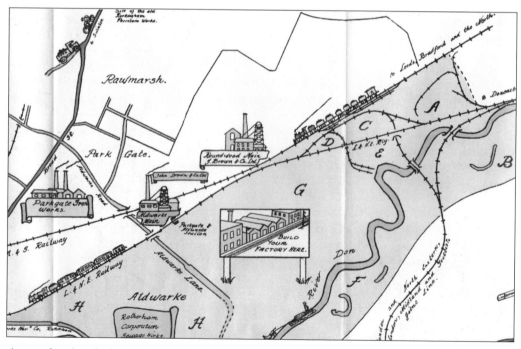

A map showing the location of Aldwarke Main, near Rotherham. Author's collection

Edward W Thirkell, mining engineer and manager. Lynn Haines

The colliery manager, Edward W Thirkell and his officials, GH Barrowclough, William Mirsby and Mr Hirst soon arrived at the pit and descended by the downcast shaft. Sunderland-born Thirkell, was an experienced and qualified mining engineer but his duties must have been stretched as he was responsible for both Car House *and* Aldwarke Main collieries. The subsequent 1911 Coal Mines Act made it illegal for a manager to be in charge of more than one colliery except with the consent of the Divisional Inspector of Mines.

When rescuers reached the cage it was a sight so dreadful that it affected them badly. This is how the *Rotherham Advertiser* reported the gruesome pit bottom scene, a few days later, on Saturday, 27 February:

The bodies were horribly shattered, and the experiences of some of the rescuers as they handled the blood-soaked clothing and crushed and bruised limbs cannot be equalled by the most gruesome incidents recorded in history as having happened either on the battlefield or in naval warfare.

Five of the eight men (Downing, Dyson, Kent, Ramsden senior and Rocket) were got out of the cage either dead or dying. Three others (Nash, Ramsden junior and Wright), 'badly mangled', were brought out alive, taken to the surface and conveyed to Rotherham General Hospital where two of them (Nash and Wright) died later the same day. The lone survivor and youngest of the victims was Arthur Ramsden, aged 24, who eventually left hospital but was described as 'a cripple' when he attending the commemorative event (see below) some eight months later. Even so, he had had a most remarkable escape, though with hardly a happy outcome. A young trammer, Arthur had descended the shaft with his late lamented collier father, Thomas Ramsden.

Under the headline, SERIOUS COLLIERY ACCIDENT/ SEVEN KILLED AT ROTHERHAM, a short account of the disaster appeared in *The Times* on the day afterwards, 24 February 1904. The pit-head was 'swarming with anxious women' and the company doctor, MC Taylor and the colliery ambulance men attended to the three 'survivors' before they were sent to hospital, 'the bodies of those killed conveyed to the unfortunate men's houses'. Ambulances had arrived from neighbouring pits: Roundwood, Car House, Warren House, and also from the adjacent Parkgate Iron and Steel Works.

William Downing, who left a widow and three young children, all girls. Rotherham Advertiser

Harry Wright, who was buried at Rawmarsh Cemetery, had only just recovered from a back injury caused when working at the colliery. Rotherham Advertiser

On the same day as *The Times*, a similar report also featured in the *Yorkshire Post*. Referring to Aldwarke as 'one of the largest South Yorkshire collieries', the locality in the aftermath of the tragedy was described in terms echoing early disasters:

Crowds of people assembled in the vicinity of the colliery immediately after the accident with the object of assuring themselves as to the safety of relatives and friends.

Mr WH Pickering, the Chief Inspector of Mines for the Yorkshire district, arrived at Aldwarke within three hours of the accident and was soon joined by assistants Mellors and Wilson. The inspectors descended the mine and examined the broken rope and smashed

The Station Hotel, close to the pit, where the inquest was held. The author

cage. Said to be about an inch thick, the rope had snapped 'practically at the same point, the cleavage being conservatively clean' (according to the *Rotherham Advertiser*, 27/2).

The inquest opened, principally for the formal identification of the deceased, at the Station Hotel, on Thursday, 25 February, before the deputy district coroner, Mr J Kenyon Parker. The colliery had already started up again, according to the next morning's edition of the *Yorkshire Post*:

> Outside the wayside hotel in which the inquest was held, there were few tokens of the grim tragedy that had occurred two mornings before. The busy colliery had lain silent and idle for a couple of days, but now the hissing of steam and the whizzing of wheels at the top of the pit told the passer by that work had again resumed. Grimy colliers returning from the coalface, pipe in mouths, and hand in pocket, lingered a moment in the cold air and then passed on, reflecting doubtless on the sad state that had overtaken their fellows, and murmuring kindly words about them and their families.

The resumed inquest began taking evidence from key witnesses on 3 March. The owners were represented by Mr W M Gichard and Mr J Raley (appointed by the Miners' Association) acted for the relatives of the deceased. The first contributor was Edward Walter Thirkell, the colliery's manager. Thirkell described how he had got news of the disaster at 6 am (he lived close by, in the grounds of the former Aldwarke Hall) and immediately went down the pit by the downcast shaft. He stated that the broken rope 'of improved plough steel' had been installed on 14 August 1902, was inspected daily and would have been replaced after two years (so the rope was just five months short of its scheduled 'use-by date'). He said that the accident may have been caused by the break being put on too suddenly or the cage 'catching and going on again', a comment perhaps not appreciated by some of the workmen.

The inquest must have been a tremendous ordeal for John Walker in particular who had twenty-eight years experience as a winding engine man at Aldwarke Main. Eighteen years earlier, in 1886, following a cage accident at Houghton Main colliery, near Barnsley, in which ten miners died, the winder there was charged with manslaughter at Leeds assizes, though found not guilty (see Volume 1). Walker stated that he noticed 'nothing wrong' with either the engine or the rope on the morning of the disaster. The only previous rope break in his time was twenty years previously when coal was being drawn. He said that he did not apply the break during the wind and the cage was let down at the usual speed.

Thomas Brameld was another key witness. His job was to examine the drawing rope which he had done – without noticing any problems – at 3 in the afternoon of the previous day.

An expert witness, Middlesbrough metallurgist John Edward Stead, FRS, said that he did not think there was any fault in the rope but that the accident was caused by 'sudden strain'. The chief mines' inspector, WH Pickering, stated that the rope may have snapped because it had been weakened by 'hidden' internal corrosion or a sudden application of the break.

In the absence of conclusive evidence, the jury's response was predictable and, apart from a somewhat vague safety recommendation, no blame was assigned to any workman, manager, official or owner:

> … the deceased lost their lives through the breaking of the rope whilst descending the Parkgate shaft, but there is not sufficient evidence to prove the cause of the rope breaking and the jury further recommend that the ropes in the upcast shaft be more frequently changed.

Samuel Featherstone, the Parkgate Labour Party pioneer, who did so much to help the families of the Aldwarke Main victims. Andrew Featherstone

The first funeral, of Thomas Ramsden, took place at Rotherham General Cemetery on the afternoon following the inquest 'in presence of a very large gathering' (*Rotherham Advertiser*, 27.2). Forty members of Aldwarke Main No 1 Branch of the Yorkshire Miners' Association marched in front of the hearse, including its Secretary, the Parkgate Labour Party pioneer Samuel Featherstone, who came to prominence when dealing with financial assistance for the bereaved families through the Workmen's Compensation Act. Featherstone was a key figure in the aftermath of the disaster, providing advice and facilitating help for five widows (two of the deceased were widowers) and thirteen young children.

Eight months after the Aldwarke disaster, on 1 October 1904, a marble plaque was unveiled in the Miners' Institute at Parkgate, the event reported in the 8 October edition of the *Rotherham Advertiser*. The memorial was funded 'without a murmur' from 'men and lads' from the colliery. A 'public tea' preceded the unveiling ceremony, which was performed – at the request of William Moulson, president of the Aldwarke branch of the Miners' Association – by the colliery's manager, Edward Thirkell. The ceremony began 'with singing of Cardinal Newman's beautiful hymn *Lead Kindly Light*', led by the Parkgate Congregational choir. The Aldwarke Miners' Association branch were represented by its president, William Moulson, Mr J Hoskin (Treasurer), Mr H Maxfield, Mr D Chapman and Samuel Featherstone (Secretary). John Wadsworth, the newly elected president of the Yorkshire Miners' Association was also in attendance and made a speech.

Details of the fatalities and injured:

William Downing, aged 30, 78 Pottery Street, Rawmarsh: a widow and three children
Mark Dyson, 48, 70 Victoria Road, Parkgate: a widow and six children
Albert Kent, 25, 40 Foljambe Road, Eastwood View, Rotherham: a widow (no children)
Martin Nash, 37, 43 Shaftsbury Square, Rotherham: a widower, three children
Thomas Ramsden, 57, 145 Nottingham Street, Rotherham: a widower (three 'grown-up' children)
Peter Rocket, 54, 55 Ashford Road, Parkgate: a widow and one child
Harry Wright, 37, 113 Beartree Road, Parkgate: widow (no children)

Seriously injured:

Arthur Ramsden, 24 (son of Thomas), 145 Nottingham Street, Rotherham: unmarried

(2) Barrow Colliery

Location: Worsbrough, Barnsley
Type: Winding accident
Fatalities: 7
Date: Friday, 15 November 1907

Speaking at the memorial unveiling ceremony for victims of the Aldwarke Main cage accident, the Yorkshire Miners' president John Wadsworth said that he 'hoped and trusted that would be the last accident of the sort they would have in the county'. Unfortunately it was not. Less than four years later another terrible cage disaster occurred at one of the largest and most modern pits in the Barnsley area.

It was late on a Friday afternoon, on a cold November day, when it happened. The day shift had long finished. A few seconds must have felt like an eternity when the double-decker cage, not dissimilar to the one at Aldwarke, stalled, shook and jolted, sending seven of its sixteen occupants to certain death and causing severe injuries to the remainder. There was no rope break or mechanical problem on this occasion so the focus of any investigation was human error.

Barrow Colliery was sunk during 1873–76 by the Barrow Haematite Iron & Steel Company Limited, so as to provide coal and coke for their ironworks at Barrow-in-Furness. The company had purchased the old Worsbrough Park mine in 1872. By the early 1900s Barrow had an output of 2,500 tons a day.

There were two downcast shafts (No 1 and No 2), each 15ft in diameter, 43 yards apart; and a third (No 3) shaft (where the accident occurred) was 17ft in diameter, located just

The 'scene of the late disaster' captured on a picture postcard. Chris & Pearl Sharp of Old Barnsley

An old iron-framed, two-decked cage, with little or no safety features in its design, c.1900. NUM

53 yards from the No 1 downcast. The No 3 shaft was brick-lined, apart from 81 yards of cast iron tubing between a depth of 69 and 150 yards. It was used exclusively for winding men to and from the Parkgate, Thorncliffe Thin and Silkstone seams, at 372, 410 and 480 yards respectively. There was a 12-inch gap between the cage and the shaft side. Hinged sheets of iron, known as flat or flag sheets were fixed to the edge of each staging and pinned to the cage, allowing the men a surface to step on when they embarked or disembarked.

At about four in the afternoon, twelve men on the upper deck and five below were being lowered from the Parkgate seam to the Thorncliffe seam, a distance of only 38 yards. This was to allow one man from the upper deck to get off. He stepped on to the landing *without waiting for the footplate to be in position.* Sixteen men therefore remained, awaiting transit. The onsetter gave the signal for the cage to be raised without making sure that everything was alright at the bottom staging. But the onsetter at the bottom staging had dropped the footplate there without telling the top onsetter. At the pit top, the engine man, in response to a signal, started raising the cage which was momentarily still attached to the shaft side. The footplate swung free so violently that it struck the girder of the Parkgate inset, and another girder, before the engine man could stop the ascent. The sudden shaking of the cage – and apparent absence of any safety gate – resulted in seven of the men (Dobson, Goodchild, Cope, Adams, Farrer, Jennings and Rooke) being flung outwards, falling to their certain death down the shaft.

The terrible situation and scene was reported in the *Yorkshire Post* the day after, 16 November 1907:

> … the officials speedily descended by another shaft. Here they met a horrible sight, the seven men being found lying lifeless, a mass of mangled humanity.

As at Aldwarke, it's hard to imagine the terrible fear that the men would have experienced for the few seconds of their 70-yard fall. But the remaining miners, though alive, must have been totally traumatized, their lamps damaged, 'imprisoned' in total darkness for almost an hour mid-shaft. The cage was gently lowered to the Parkgate level, the men extracted and conveyed to the pit-top via one of the downcast shafts. The rescue party was led by the pit manager, Mr WR Steele. At the surface Dr Burnham and the ambulance men did what they could to administer first aid but three of the party (Wigglesworth, Hoddle and Sanderson) were so badly injured they were taken to Barnsley Beckett Hospital, where they were treated for fractured legs and concussion. A man at the pit bottom who had witnessed the dreadful scene there was so shocked he was said to have 'cried like a child' and was 'incapable of giving any account of what he had seen'.

The bodies of the accident victims were placed in a cabin, where most of them were identified by distraught friends and relatives who were also employed at the colliery. Four of the dead were taken to the Mason's Arms at Worsbrough Dale, to await the coroner's inquest.

Again, the *Yorkshire Post*, provided a rapid overview of the increasingly grim pit top scene:

> The news of the affair quickly spread, and the greatest anxiety prevailed in Worsbrough and Barnsley, where so many of the men live. Crowds gathered at the pit hill to await the sad news, and crowds of men, women and children lined the streets awaiting the latest findings.

The report included a remarkable interview with one of the survivors, a young lad called George Hargreaves, aged 'about 19':

> Someone rapped and the cage went up. It was then that I felt the cage go on one side, and we did not know what had happened. I think the men must have fallen out soon after we left the Thorncliffe seam. We could get no replies to our shouting; our lamps were put out by the vibration, and we lay together in the cage, which, after being

Worsbrough village was packed with people paying their respects when the funeral of several of the Barrow Colliery victims took place on 19 November 1907. The scene was recorded on this photographic postcard. Author's collection

stopped, appeared to be in a tilted position. It was three-quarters of an hour before we were lowered and rescued. It was a fearful time. I said my prayers in the cage.

As one would expect, at the first opportunity, on 23 November 1907, a detailed account of the Barrow cage disaster was published in the *Barnsley Chronicle*. Pictures of all seven victims appeared, probably the first time that actual photographs of multiple mine disaster victims had been published in the town's newspaper; and proceedings from the inquest, which had opened in the Mitchell Memorial Hall, Worsbrough Dale, on the Monday (18 November), were reported.

The *Chronicle* also provided human interest stories concerning several of the victims. Goodchild left a widow and six children, one of them 'a cripple'. Farrer would have been celebrating his 21st birthday on the Saturday and his mother was actually making preparations when 'mournful tidings arrived'. Right-back for Worsbrough Bridge Wesleyan Reform Football Club, his team cancelled their fixture in respect of their friend's death. Cope, also a local footballer, was engaged to be married at Christmas. His mother was a widow, her husband killed in an accident at Swaithe Main colliery sixteen years previously. Rooke had stopped to talk to a friend, delaying his ascent on the previous draw, therefore entering the fateful cage.

One young miner came to the cabin where several of the bodies were taken. Recognising one of them as his best mate, the lad threw himself down on his knees, 'kissed the dead face' and burst into tears. The two friends had been working together that very afternoon.

The funerals of Goodchild and Cope, at St Thomas', Worsbrough Dale and Farrer and Rooke, at St Mary's in Worsbrough village, attracted a gathering of mourners not seen since the Swaithe Main disaster of 1875. The crowd was said to be so dense at Worsbrough Dale that the tram service was suspended for two hours. 'Touching scenes' were also reported at Hoyland and Dodworth where Dobson and Jennings were buried, respectively; and also at Barnsley Cemetery when Adams was interred.

As at Aldwarke, His Majesty's Chief Inspector of Mines for the Yorkshire and Lincolnshire District, Mr WH Pickering, represented the Government at the inquest. John Wadsworth (now an MP) was in attendance and the Yorkshire Miners Association were represented by their new young president, the soon to be legendary Herbert Smith, assisted by Levi Dickinson. The mine's manager, William Rodley Steel, was also present as was the colliery company's agent, Ralph Richardson. Mr PP Maitland was the coroner.

The first day was concerned with the formal evidence of identification, which understandably proved to be very upsetting for the widows, mothers and fathers of the deceased; and especially difficult when detailed medical evidence was provided by Dr HAL Banham. Messages of sympathy were expressed on behalf of the principal representatives referred to above.

The adjourned inquest, held on 28 November, included eyewitness, specialist and professional evidence; and cross-examination took place concerning the possible cause or causes of the disaster. A 'fine large model' of the No 3 upcast shaft was placed before the jury and 'an exact model' of the cage – after it had been damaged – was provided by the mines inspector. Steel, the colliery manager, was first to give evidence, explaining that he had never known any difficulty in the use of the flagsheets by which the men got from the cage to the roadways and that all machinery was in good working order. The engineman at the No 3 shaft, George Henry Anderson, said that he had been at Barrow only three months but had thirteen years winding experience at other pits. He confirmed that the winding machinery and signaling apparatus was in order on the day of the accident. He described starting to wind up the cage on a signal until he heard, after six or seven revolutions, 'a noise on the drum as if something had slipped'. The two hangers-on, Waring and Weldrick, the men responsible for attaching the flagsheets, were questioned and there was controversy concerning their conflicting evidence. Waring, in particular, was accused of giving false testimony by the coroner.

WH Pickering, the experienced mines inspector, felt certain that the disaster was caused by the flagsheet not being off when the cage re-started, and that if a warning signal had been given immediately, the engineman could have stopped it. He concluded that both onsetters were 'to blame…for both were in too great a hurry to get the cage away'. He also stated that, although the rope, capping and shaft fitting 'were in excellent condition and of first class materials', saving the lives of the rest of the men, even more lives would have been saved if the cage had been fitted with 'properly designed gates'.

The inquest met again, on 4 December, this time at Barnsley's town hall and, after six or seven hours of hearing evidence, the jury returned the following verdict:

That the seven men met their deaths through negligence, being thrown out of the cage to the shaft bottom, owing to the flat sheet being fast on the lower deck when the cage was signalled off. The two hangers-on were guilty of carelessness and negligence, but not criminal negligence, and are very censurable.

This photographic montage relating to the Barrow disaster was created and published by Warner Gothards of Barnsley, specialists in producing disaster postcards. A similar reconstruction appeared in the news magazine, The Penny Illustrated Paper. *Author's collection*

The coroner agreed that the verdict was correct and was very critical of Waring and Weldrick, the two negligent hangers-on. A formal inquiry (under Section 45 of the 1887 Coal Mines Regulation Act) into the Barrow disaster was conducted by Professor Richard AS Redmayne of the new University of Birmingham. Redmayne, who became Britain's first chief inspector of mines in 1908 and a key figure in the 1912 Cadeby disaster, confirmed the inquest findings, the accident being a consequence of 'carelessness and hurry on the part of the two onsetters'.

The end of the cages were subsequently fitted with safety gates, something that the agent had apparently planned to do anyway – but that was little consolation for the bereaved families.

Details of the dead, injured and those 'unhurt' were:

William Adams (also known as Slack), aged 28, brakesman, married, 62 Oxford Street, Barnsley
Frank Dobson, 40, chargeman of the staple pit, married, Dick Croft, Hoyland
Isaac Farrer, 20, haulage man, 33 George Street, Worsbrough Bridge
Walter Lewis Goodchild, 35, hanger-on, married, 8 Hammerton's Buildings, Worsbrough Dale
Thomas William Jennings, 18, haulage lad, 2 Powell Street, Worsbrough Dale
Thomas Rathmell Cope, 23, hanger-on, 30 Jarratt's Buildings, Worsbrough Dale
Byas Rooke, 22, haulage man, 120 High Street, Worsbrough Dale

Seriously injured:

George Hoddle, James Street, Worsbrough Dale (fractured leg and other injuries)
Herbert Sanderson, James Street, Worsbrough Bridge (severe scalp wound).
Charles Wigglesworth, 45, 3 Commercial Street, Barnsley (fractured leg and scalp wound)

Slightly injured:

John Galvin, Barnsley
Arthur Fleetwood, High Street, Worsbrough Dale
Bernard Kilroy, Barnsley

Unhurt:

George Hargreaves, Marriott's Terrace, Worsbrough Bridge
Gilbert Jackson, Clarkson Street, Worsbrough Dale
Joe Ormston, Worsbrough Dale

A moving ceremony took place at Birdwell, not far from old Barrow Colliery, on Saturday 15 November 2007, to commemorate the centenary of the disaster. Planned and organised by the local residents' action group, a cherry tree was planted by the Mayor of Barnsley (and retired miner), Councillor Len Picken and the local MP, Michael Clapham. A small plaque was also unveiled, the whole dedicated by Canon Ron Thomson and Rev John Bellfield. Several descendants of the accident victims were in attendance, as was the Barrow miners' banner and representatives from the National Union of Mineworkers.

The service of remembrance, tree planting and dedication, on the centenary of the Barrow cage disaster, Birdwell, 17 November 1907. The Mayor of Barnsley, Councillor Len Picken, was in attendance, as was Mick Clapham MP, representatives from the NUM, the local community and several descendants of those who died. The author

(3) Hoyland Silkstone Colliery

Location: Platts Common, Barnsley
Type: Underground boiler explosion
Fatalities: 4
Date: Saturday, 23 November 1907

Only eight days after the Barrow disaster and less than a mile away, a serious accident occurred at Hoyland Silkstone colliery. Although not classed as a disaster, the circumstances and events relating to the event attracted widespread public and media interest, especially due to the heroism of one of the miners involved: Mr Francis Chandler, who became the first recipient of the King Edward Medal.

The colliery was owned and operated by the Hoyland Silkstone Coal & Coke Company Limited, from land owned by Earl Fitzwilliam and TFC Vernon-Wentworth. There were three shafts, known as the Flockton, Silkstone and Thorncliffe, the first two functioning as downcasts, the third as an upcast.

The accident occurred late on a Saturday night when seven men were making repairs to the roof over the boiler house which was 'in steam' in the pit bottom of the Parkgate seam. A large girder weighing over a ton was in process of being placed in a position to give greater support to the roof but collapsed on top of the boiler, followed by hundreds of tons of debris. Pipes from the boiler broke and hot steam added to the hazardous situation. Greenwood Ogden, a ripper, was killed outright, having been struck by the iron girder and the others: Arthur Cooke, Walter Sistern, brothers Lawrence and Leonard Chandler, Francis ('Frank')

End of the day shift at Hoyland Silkstone Colliery, from an Edwardian postcard, c.1907. Norman Ellis collection

The distinctive face of Frank Chandler who became a local celebrity and national hero following his brave exploits at Hoyland Silkstone Colliery in 1907. Author's collection

Chandler (their father, who was a deputy, in charge of the men) and Isaac Scawthorpe, suffered injuries and severe burns. A brief report of the accident quickly appeared in *The Times* of 25 November and, on the same day, more detailed accounts were published in the regional press. The *Yorkshire Post*, for example, described the bravery of Chandler senior:

> … a deputy, Frank Chandler … was able to reach the pit bottom close by, and his shouts were heard in the seam below. The cage came to the Parkgate seam and apparently Chandler, despite his injuries, was able to get into the cage [after crawling along the roadway] and signal. He was brought to the surface, where he was able to tell what had happened.

As a result of Chandler's heroics, all the men were rescued, though sadly Cooke, Leonard Chandler and Sistern succumbed, in Barnsley Beckett Hospital, a few days later.

Details of the dead and injured were published as follows:

Dead
Leonard Chandler, 19 (son of Frank), trammer, Church Street, Jump
Arthur Cooke, 33, ripper, Bells Yard / Queen Street, Hoyland Common
Greenwood Ogden (initially some news reports give his age as 55 but more likely it
    was 38), ripper, Church Street, Jump
Walter Sistern, 32, ripper, Sales Street / Tinker Lane, Hoyland Common

Injured
Frank Chandler, deputy, Church Street, Jump
Lawrence Chandler (son of Frank), rope lad, Church Street, Jump
Isaac Scawthorpe (Scothorne or Scothorn in some accounts, son-in-law of Frank), dataller, Church Street, Jump. The unfortunate Scawthorpe was not an official member of the working party but a Rockingham miner, observing the operations.

In Memoriam of

Greenwood Ogden,
AGED 38 YEARS,

Arthur Cooke,
AGED 33 YEARS,

Leonard Chandler, & Walter Sistern,
AGED 19 YEARS,
AGED 35 YEARS,

Who were all engaged in Repairing a Boiler House in the mine of

The hoyland Silkstone Colliery.

ON SATURDAY, NOV. 23rd, 1907,

When a heavy fall of the Roof killed G. OGDEN on the spot.
A. COOKE died in the Hospital on the Sunday. L. CHANDLER on
the Wednesday, and W. SISTERN on the Friday following.

Faithful below they did their duty—
Leave unto the Lord the rest.

This memorial card to the four victims of the Hoyland Silkstone accident is evocative of others produced in Victorian times. Author's collection

Chandler in Buckingham Palace, respectfully receiving his medal from his lookalike, Edward VII. Author's collection

The inquest was held at Barnsley Town Hall, coroner Mr PP Maitland presiding. The HM Inspector of Mines for Yorkshire and Lincolnshire, WH Pickering, was in attendance, along with other representatives, including solicitors J Hewitt and J Raley for the colliery company and the miners respectively. After adjournment, further meetings took place at the old school in Jump and, finally, back at the town hall. However, because Ogden's death came under the jurisdiction of the Sheffield coroner, a separate inquest for him was held at Hoyland, though agreement was reached to have a common verdict for all four of the deceased.

In his summing up, the coroner spoke about the 'great bravery' of Frank Chandler and said that he would be prepared to recommend that he should receive the new Edward Medal, sentiments also shared by the jury. A verdict of 'accidental death' was given for the deceased men and the colliery manager was held responsible (though not criminally) for the girders being not of sufficient strength to withstand the weight of the roof.

Frank Chandler (looking extremely like the King) was the first of two miners (the other being 35-year-old Welsh collier Henry Everson) who received the medal from His Majesty Edward VII, at a special ceremony in Buckingham Palace, on Thursday, 27 February 1908. The previous evening Chandler was given a VIP meal in the House of Commons, followed by an evening of entertainment at the Pavilion Music Hall. There was comprehensive news coverage in the *Barnsley Chronicle* who dispatched a representative to London for the occasion.

A great celebratory dinner in Chandler's honour was held on 1 March in Hoyland Common. For many years afterwards, Frank Chandler appears to have enjoyed his celebrity status locally, proud to wear his medal as he walked around Jump and Hoyland. My great friend the Hoyland Common local historian (and former Hoyland Silkstone and Rockingham miner) Arthur Clayton, who died aged 101 in 2002, often recalled Chandler and his fame; and also remembered a victim of the disaster, Chandler's son-in-law, Walter Sistern, who as a young man fought in the Boer War and later lodged with Clayton's mother. Several years ago, when giving a talk to a men's group at Snaith I met the great grandson of Frank Chandler, who told me that he had the medal prior to its sale.

The Edward Medal was instituted by Royal Warrant on 13 July 1907, to recognize acts of bravery of miners and quarrymen and became known as 'the miners' VC'. An amendment was made in order to allow the medal to be awarded to all industrial workers in factory accidents and disasters, two years later. There were, therefore, 'Mines' and 'Industry' versions. The medal had two grades: first-class (silver) and second-class (bronze). In 1971, surviving recipients were invited to exchange their award for the George Cross, a small number declining. Only 77 silver and 320 bronze have been awarded, making it one of the rarer gallantry awards.

Two serious accidents, albeit ones not involving a large loss of life, occurred within a few months of each other, in 1910, at John Brown's Rotherham Main colliery at Canklow. The first, an explosion of gas, occurred on a busy afternoon shift in the hot and over 600 yards deep Parkgate seam, at 8.30 pm, on 21 July, where miners often worked in a near naked condition. One man, Reginald Evans, died and six others were burnt, three of of them so badly that they were described in the *Rotherham Advertiser* as 'seriously injured'; one of the latter, Albert Fletcher, being in a 'precarious' condition. The second accident took place in the early morning of Monday, 12 December, during drilling operations. A fall of stone buried several men, killing a father and son (Ted and Wilfred Rose) and injuring two others.

Part Two

The Cadeby Tragedy
1912

"It was like a door shutting with a great amount of pressure behind it and the roar came afterwards…Mr Bury shouted 'Down on your faces lads' …"

Percy Murgatroyd, a survivor

During the first decade or so of the new century, South Yorkshire had not witnessed what might be regarded as a major mining disaster for over thirty years, since Swaithe Main in 1875, when 143 men and boys were killed. There was certainly little evidence of complacency though, in the context of very serious accidents in other, albeit more distant regions, most notably at Senghenydd and Wattstown in south Wales (1901 and 1905, 81 and 119 dead); Maypole, Wigan (1908, 75 dead); West Stanley, Durham (1909, 168 dead); Wellington, Whitehaven (136 dead); and the terrible toll of death at Hulton, Lancashire in 1910 when, just a few days before Christmas, 344 perished in a single explosion, the third most serious pit disaster in British history. Closer to home, at Micklefield in West Yorkshire, the Peckfield explosion of 1896 left 65 dead and remained Yorkshire's last major disaster, until the Cadeby tragedy of 1912. William Henry Pickering, the much respected HM Inspector of Mines for the Yorkshire and the North Midland District, in 1911 wrote in what was to be his last report:

> The last disaster was 1896, a remarkable record for a district where most of the persons employed work in very fiery mines … It is very encouraging to note a substantial reduction of the number of accidents, the number of deaths, and in the death-rate per 1000 persons employed … the lowest for the past 11 years.

Locally, three men lost their lives whilst shot-firing in an explosion at Barnsley Main colliery, at 4am, on Saturday, 6 July 1912. Mines inspector WH Pickering attended the first day of the inquest, held on the following Monday, 8 July, when 'distressing scenes were witnessed' while bodies were identified. The deceased, who died of severe burns and carbon monoxide poisoning, were Walter Jepson (aged 46), a deputy, 25 Doncaster Road, Ardsley; Thomas Hunt (49), coal-cutting machine man, 26 Osborne Street, Barnsley; and Thomas Eltoft (38), coal-cutting machine man, 24 Waltham Street, Barnsley.

Then, the next day, a grim Tuesday, 9 July 1912, the most tragic disaster in modern South Yorkshire coalmining history occurred at Cadeby Main, situated near the ancient 'king's stronghold' of Conisbrough, where George V and Queen Mary had been welcomed by cheering residents and schoolchildren a day earlier. Inspector Pickering, himself an Edward Medal recipient, awarded for gallantry at Water Haigh Colliery (Oulton, Leeds) just two years earlier, was one of the 88 official fatalities, killed in a second explosion which

Respect being shown for the victims of the 1912 Cadeby disaster during the Cadeby Miners' Gala event, 31 May 2009, organised by artist Rachel Horne (centre). A symbolic wreath was laid at the gravestone of Samuel Thomas Sanders, aged 51, who lost his life during the rescue operations.

accounted for 53 deaths, including two of his colleagues and the managers of both Cadeby and Denaby collieries.

The unfolding drama of Cadeby, in the context of the royal visit and the 'high status' deaths of colliery and government officials, undoubtedly enhanced national and indeed international media interest. Editors and journalists were quick to report the fact that the royal party had diverted to Cadeby on the evening of the 9th and that the king's presence had 'saved lives' due to 'holiday-making' miners not working on the fateful nightshift. The king was even praised for his bravery, making an underground visit to Elsecar Colliery, on 11 July, 'despite the nearby explosion' of the previous day. But, it is also clear from many contemporary reports, that the royals were genuinely shocked and 'much distressed' (eg *The Times*, 10 July 1912) by their unscheduled but requested visit to Cadeby Main.

(4) Cadeby Main

Location: near Conisbrough Railway Station and Cadeby village, Doncaster
Type: Two explosions
Fatalities: 88*
Date: Tuesday, 9 July 1912

The Denaby Main Colliery Company Limited began sinking a sister colliery, to be known as Cadeby Main (after the rural village nearby) in 1889, both concerns forming the Denaby & Cadeby Main Collieries Co Ltd, in 1893. The two pits were little more than a mile apart but Cadeby became a frontier colliery, the most easterly and deepest in Yorkshire. There were two shafts, 87 yards apart. The downcast, known as No 1 Eastern, was 752 yards deep and the upcast or No 2 Western reached 738 yards. The famous Barnsley seam was the only coal worked, entirely 'by hand'. It was a lucrative strata but well known to be gassy and liable to spontaneous combustion in certain conditions, therefore had to be managed with great care.

Prior to 1912, the new Cadeby colliery had in fact experienced 35 underground fires, but only one fatal explosion, on 11 March 1899, when two men lost their lives. Persistent gob fires had been troublesome in the South District, near the faults and junction with Denaby Main. On 12 January 1912, four men received 'slight burns' following a 'small explosion of gas' from a fire discovered in November. Further fiery instances were reported on 2 February and 10 April, by a deputy, James Springthorpe and chargeman/dataller, Sanders, who was to lose his life in the second explosion.

Cadeby's most senior man was its managing director, William H Chambers, who was also a qualified mining engineer and played an active role in the management of the colliery. But he was in Sunderland when the pit fired. His nephew, Douglas Chambers, who managed Denaby Main colliery, lost his life in the second explosion. Harry S Witty, the agent for both collieries, had previously managed Cadeby. Under Witty, the Cadeby manager was Charles Barry, who was assisted by under-managers Cusworth and Croxhall. Although brought out alive, Barry became a fatal victim of the second explosion, when he died in Fullerton hospital.

The Spring of 1912 was a particularly difficult time for communities in and around Conisbrough and Denaby Main colliery village, where the most of the Cadeby men lived. The minimum wage strike, which had began on 1 March (the first truly national miners'

Detail from a picture postcard showing the ever-growing Cadeby crowd 'waiting for news'. Author's collection

Doncaster Road, Denaby Main, captured by a local photographer in about 1905. Chris & Pearl Sharp/Old Barnsley

strike), lasted for six hard weeks. When the men did returned to work it was amid a cloud of uncertainty and they found the pit in too bad a condition for coal to be drawn.

No doubt there were still bitter memories too, of the vindictive Denaby Main evictions of January 1903 when families were forced out of their homes, many of them having to live outdoors in tents. Later, Reverend Jesse Wilson described some of the dreadful scenes in a book, *The Story of the Great Struggle, 1902–3* (1904), including the following:

> There the brave little woman with her ten children stood in the street beside their scraps of furniture, houseless and homeless, with nowhere to go … the sight has haunted me ever since.

It was not the first time (for example, in 1877 and 1885) that the colliery company had used its position as a major owner of its workers' houses as the most cruel of sanctions during an industrial dispute. The owners were well known for their hardline stances against their employees and anti-union attitudes, wanting total control at all times.

As at other neighbouring pits, and despite improved regional statistics, serious accidents at Cadeby *were* regular occurrences. During the five years before 1912 there were 30 fatalities, at least five every year. Funerals of miners were therefore commonplace, undertakers kept busy and purveyors of mourning attire thrived. Most fatalities were due to roof falls and haulage mishaps. In the months just before the disaster, Walter Hall, a 17-year-old electrician, was killed, when he fell over a girder (11 January) and a filler, George William Philips, aged 29, lost his life after being struck by a prop.

George V and one of the ladies-in-waiting at Conisbrough Castle. Author's collection

The disaster

The following narrative of the events of 8/9 July is based on official sources, contemporary newspaper reports and personal reminiscence. Catherine Bailey, in her recent (2007) and much acclaimed *Black Diamonds* book, also provides us with an excellent interpretation of the Cadeby disaster in the context of the royal visit.

Monday, 8 July was a warm, pleasant morning and many of the houses and streets in Conisbrough and Denaby Main village had a colourful air, decorated with red, white and blue flags in readiness for the visit of King George V and Queen Mary to the ancient castle. Local schools closed for a day or half-day and many residents enjoyed a day off work or domestic chores. Edward Thompson (born 1904) recalled his impressions of the occasion when he was a pupil at Morley Place School:

> We were soon marshalled into a procession, headed by Mr W Smith and assisted by [our] teachers. We marched … to the castle grounds. the sloping bank to the left side of the entrance had been kept as a reserve for the boys and girls of Morley Place and we were arranged to stand in four rows. The open space in front of us was tightly packed with both residents and visitors … The courtyard was kept private as it was to be the place where their Majesties were to take afternoon tea.
>
> Much happiness prevailed in the dense crowd during the waiting period … it was a happy crowd … but suddenly there was silence, for the arrival of their Majesties was imminent. They entered through the castle gate to be greeted by a wonderful ovation … I had a good view of them. The King, a bearded man, was wearing a fawn coloured robe. Their Majesties stood for a short while to listen to a song of welcome from the scholars, and then … moved … to take tea … It was a day of great joy.

Later that evening the royals and guests were provided with a banquet of thirteen courses, seven miles away, in the State Dining Room at Wentworth House, hosted by 'Billy', 7th Earl Fitzwilliam and his wife, Lady Maud. As they prepared for bed and an early start, which included a visit to Silverwood Colliery, mothers and wives in Conisbrough and Denaby were preparing 'snaps' and water or tea bottles for their sons and husbands, due to start the night or 'repair' shift at Cadeby Main.

The 'repairing' (non-coal-getting) night shift always started at 10 pm and lasted until 6 am, deputies going down with the men in the first 'draw' as usual. But there was a very light attendance due to the evening's royal celebrations. Only 112 men turned up to work underground, little over 20 per cent of the normal shift size.

The first indication that something was not right occurred during the early hours of Tuesday morning, towards the end of the shift. Albert Wildman, of Ivanhoe Road, Conisbrough and William Humphries, who lived at Annerley Street in Denaby Main, were paired with each other, well away from their normal coalfaces and their usual mates who were not working. They were on their own, laying a road in the No 1 district, a distant and lonely part of the pit at the best of times and even more so on this fragmented shift. A 'sudden stoppage of air' was an obvious warning sign, followed by 'a warm heat which travelled past me' ('a puff of air' in some reports), according to Humphries. When the air 'came back' (reversal) he could see that it 'picked up dust'. An experienced miner with seventeen years experience at Cadeby, Humphries sought help, walking to the pit bottom where he told two men working there about his concerns. It was about 2 am. Nothing resolved, but understandably anxious, he returned to Wildman but they were soon joined by Joseph Farmer, who feared that there had been an explosion in the South Plane. Thirty minutes after the first alarm, Farmer went to investigate and his worst fears were confirmed.

After a couple of hundred yards there were obvious signs of an explosion, including damaged tubs, girders and very foul air. His shouts in the dark received no response. Then, the two lonely datallers were reinforced by a small party consisting of Jack Bullock, Sylvester and Nicholson and cautious searching began. Nicholson and Wildman went to

Mines rescue men from the Wath Main station were summoned to Cadeby. Author's collection

find an official, locating a deputy, George Fisher, who joined them at about 4.55am. The body of Martin Mulrooney, a Mexborough dataller, was found. William Humphries was dispatched to the pit bottom to get rescue assistance and Fisher began an inspection but his light was extinguished (by the afterdamp) when testing for gas. On his way to the pit bottom Humphries met Herbert Cusworth, an under-manager and James Springthorpe.

The Denaby and Cadeby rescue team had assembled as quickly as possible but it was almost 6 am before they were able to descend the pit. Meanwhile, the Wath Mines Rescue Station had dispatched a team of men and breathing equipment. Surprisingly, the rest of the miners, 76 in total, had been allowed to work on until the shift finished at 6 am. The colliery pay shed (or pay station) was made available as a temporary mortuary. Twenty 'crowd members' volunteered at the request of manager/agent Witty to go down the pit and carry out the bodies. Mines inspectors Pickering, Hewitt and Tickle had arrived at the colliery not long after 9 am and also went underground, joining pit managers Chambers, Barry and under-managers Cusworth and Croxhall, several deputies and various rescue team members plus volunteers. Two other mines inspectors, Wilson (Pickering's senior inspector) and Hudspeth (for Leeds and Doncaster), arrived later but wisely decided to study the plans of the South District before descending. This saved their lives. By mid morning 22 bodies had been recovered.

Then the unthinkable happened. James Springthorpe, who was at level No 14, later described how he had heard a 'rushing noise' and had just time to shout, 'Look out Herbert' to Littlewood, who was nearby, when he was 'knocked about' and his lamp 'knocked out of his hand'. The air was foul and full of dust. The second explosion trapped many of the men behind a massive roof fall, the afterdamp accounting for most of the 53 fatalities. Only Winch and Lawrence survived from the Denaby and Cadeby Rescue team.

Agent Harry Witty's grim description of his experiences after descending the pit following the second explosion, included the following:

> I met several men who had been slightly injured. [James] Springthorpe was one of these and Harold Booth. The others were only slightly touched. I met others coming from where the explosion had been. I met Mr Hudspeth first and we examined the return and found the stuff coming from there very foul. It smelt strongly of gasolene or benzoline … We went lower down and found a road had been made over a fall. I went through there and found Mr Wilson paying attention to some of the injured … I went then on to 14s level and … I went higher up to No 19s landing and found bodies in a cluster … I saw Douglas Chambers and then in front of him Mr Pickering and on his right Mr Hewitt and Mr Tickle. In front of Mr Pickering, with his feet under Mr Pickering's head, was Mr Bury … the bodies were somewhat discoloured by dust but there was no signs of burning …

A vivid account of the second explosion was recalled by another survivor, Percy Murgatroyd:

> It was like a door shutting with a great amount of pressure behind it and the roar came afterwards … Mr Bury shouted 'Down on your faces lads'. I think they knew what it was … when I came to my senses I turned the oxygen on and got the tubes in my mouth and I suppose I went straight to the crossgate … After I came to I heard someone say something, Ben Ward, Albert Farmery and Tom Stribley. They said: 'Let's get hold of each other's hands, we will die together …

William Chambers, the D&CC managing director, had arrived at Cadeby from Sunderland at about 3.20 pm and, after discussions with colleagues, concluded that there was no one left in the workings of the South District. Arrangements to build brick stoppings in order to isolate the 14 and 23 levels were then made, a task involving 20 men. Chambers then met the most senior government official responsible for safety in mines: Richard Redmayne, the Chief Inspector, who had now arrived at the scene (and lodged at Chambers' house). Interestingly, in his autobiography, Redmayne mentions that on his arrival he was given a telegram, sent on behalf of the Home Secretary (Reginal McKenna), ordering him not to descend the mine 'unless absolutely necessary'. As if to emphasise the warning, about 3.30 the next morning, a third, relatively small explosion occurred, blowing down part of the stoppings and sending the men running for their lives, two or three of them suffering from the effects of the deadly afterdamp. A few hours later the stoppings were replaced and the danger area *apparently* resealed.

Informed at breakfast of the first explosion, the King, through his Private Secretary, sent a telegram expressing his and the Queen's shock and sending condolences to the affected families and sufferers, before embarking on a busy morning schedule of visits. It was whilst the royal party were at lunch, as guests of Lord Halifax, at Hickleton Hall, that news came through of the second explosion and increased death toll. The King ignored advice to abandon his planned descent of Elsecar pit in the afternoon, keen to 'see for myself … the risks to which my miners are exposed'. Bound for the comforts of Wentworth, a brief unscheduled visit to Cadeby by George V and Queen Mary took place at about 7.30 pm, summarized in the *Mexborough & Swinton Times* a few days later, as follows:

> The King looked pale and sorrowful as he appeared with the Queen at the top of the colliery steps, and the Queen, without restraint at all, shed the tears of a mother, a wife, and a daughter.

Edward Thompson, who was a boy of eight years old, recalled seeing the King and Queen arrive at Cadeby:

> There was a large crowd of people present who waved and raised their hats but there were no cheers, just silence and tear-stained faces.

The *Times* reporter concluded that the 'epoch-making' visit 'will make a magnificent piece of twentieth-century history'. Ninety-five years later, *Black Diamonds* author Catherine Bailey balances the media euphoria surrounding the unexpected royal visit to a letter written shortly afterwards by the King to Billy Fitzwilliam (and also one sent by the Queen to the Archbishop of York), in which the Cadeby disaster was not mentioned: '… it was as if it had never happened'.

News coverage

The first printed accounts of the disaster were widely reported in the national and regional press, on 10 and 11 July. *The Times* report almost covered three columns under the headline of PIT DISASTER IN YORKSHIRE and alongside it was THE KING IN A PIT, an account of the royal visit, up to the descent of Elsecar colliery. The newspaper's own 'correspondents', almost certainly Mexborough area journalists, included Edward (sic)

How The Times *newspaper announced the Cadeby disaster to its readers.* The Times

PIT DISASTER IN YORKSHIRE.

GREAT LOSS OF LIFE.

MINE INSPECTORS AMONG THE VICTIMS.

THE KING AND QUEEN VISIT THE SCENE.

A terrible colliery accident occurred yesterday in the heart of the Yorkshire mining district, which the King and Queen are now visiting. Early in the morning an explosion took place in the south-west portion of the Cadeby main pit, and of the 32 men at work there all but two were killed.

Later in the day, while a rescue party was below in the workings, another explosion, or series of explosions, took place, as a result of which the initial death-roll was more than doubled. Up to a late hour last night 74 were known to be dead, and it was feared that this total would eventually be exceeded.

The following who were members of the

The drama unfolds in the local media: headlines from the Mexborough and Swinton Times. Mexborough and Swinton Times

SATURDAY, JULY 13, 1912

Terrible Pit Calamity at Cadeby

Series of Explosions Sweep the Mine.

Heavy Death Roll.   Eighty-Six Lives Lost.

HEROIC RESCUERS KILLED INSTANTLY.

Mines Inspectors and Mine Managers among the Victims.

Official List of Killed and Injured.

King and Queen Visit the Colliery.

Pen Picture of Memorable Scenes.

Inquest Opened.   The Funeral Arrangements.

RELIEF FUND OPENED.

£1,500 ALREADY SUBSCRIBED.

Mr. F. J. O. MONTAGU'S Spontaneous Generosity.

(BY OUR OWN REPORTER).

Humphries' 'survivor's account' and Percy Murgatroyd's graphic description of the second explosion. The main report even included the royal party's evening visit to Cadeby – extremely fast publishing by any standards. The *Manchester Guardian* report was particularly eloquent, and included the following:

The Cadeby mine is in the beautiful valley of the Dearne. The colliery itself is an ugly object but it does not spoil either the colour or the sweeping configuration or the country around. All day today rooks have been flying over the colliery yard, flying down on heaps of shale, then sailing off to the elms across the valley. The two winding wheels revolve steadily and by and by on the gangway emerged a little group, six men feeling their way down among them, a little smear of colour – a blue bed spread on a stretcher. Then the crowd on the road lost them, recovering them to sight in the colliery yard below as they passed behind a brick building … This was repeated again and again.

The weekly newspapers included very detailed reports about the disaster and its aftermath. There was comprehensive coverage – three full pages – in the *Mexborough and Swinton Times*, published on Saturday, 13 July, probably the first source of information for local families. Under the headline 'Terrible Pit Calamity at Cadeby' was the story of the two explosions, 'heroic rescuers', 'stories from survivors', the opening of the inquest, funeral arrangements and the opening of a relief fund. On the second page, alongside the official list of victims, their ages and addresses, is a photographic montage of 32 of the VICTIMS and HEROES and above it four images of the OFFICIALS OF THE DENABY AND CADEBY COLLIERIES (WH Chambers, HS Witty, Charles Bury and Douglas Chambers [nephew of WH]. The previous page also has photographs of 'the crowd anxiously waiting for news', an image which was to be repeated on several picture postcards; and a picture of the rescue team. Small portraits of two of the government mines inspectors who were killed – WH Pickering and RH Hewitt – also appeared. All in all, it is a very substantial record of the disaster and its immediate aftermath and had some exclusiveness too. The unnamed *Times* reporter appears to have been the first pressman to obtain 'a reliable account of the tragedy', by interviewing William Humphries. The resultant information was used by other newspapers, including the *Rotherham Advertiser*, though in the course of transfer, Humphries' forename was wrongly copied as 'Edward'.

The eyewitness reports in the *Mexborough & Swinton Times* still make compelling reading, even allowing for the journalistic style of the day. Here, for example, is a short piece about the bringing out of the dead, seen by the burgeoning crowd on the Tuesday evening:

At nine o'clock began the ghastly procession of the dead. Slowly and reverently they were carried out of the pit-mouth down the long galleries in full view of the thousands of alarmed onlookers. From seven o'clock until nine the great crowds had gradually accumulated in the roads leading to the pit-yard, but all was perfectly quiet then, for no one knew anything definite. People merely amused themselves with conjecture and were inclined to regard the rumoured explosion as another of the mare's nests for which colliery explosions are often taken as fitting subjects. But the appearance of that first corpse on the top of the tall gantry was enough for the onlookers. A gasp of horror flew around, and swift as the message of the beacon light, the whole of the district was apprised of the horror within their midst.

After contrasting the royal celebrations of the previous day, the writer continued his description of the grim scene as his Victorian predecessors had often done; and was able to give, even if an over-estimate, an indication of the immense size of the crowd that had assembled:

> Here was a cold shudder in the air, and a whisper of death in the wind. The crowd, which had flocked into the place from miles around in the heat of the afternoon grew and swelled until at seven o'clock there must have been not less than eighty thousand. Every one was a mourner, and in all that multitude scarcely a sound seemed to be raised. Everywhere was grey stolid grief and only when you mingled … did you detect the soft weeping of a widow, and there the low fearful muttering of a father whose strong bright son was no more. Anything more impressive and depressing one could not well imagine.

We are also provided with a glimpse of the village of Denaby Main a day after the disaster:

> Up one street and down another you saw nothing but the hideous monotony of drawn blinds and women standing discussing the accident in the street, relieved in sinister fashion here and there by the sight of a coffin being transferred from the colliery ambulance into the house, or by overhearing hackneyed street-door philosophy.

The writer then went on to describe 'one little incident' in which a young press photographer, 'sensing only a startling picture', pointed his camera at three weeping women on the station footbridge, after they had identified bodies of loved ones at the pay station 'mortuary'. The incensed crowd 'promptly smashed his camera, and nearly smashed him'.

Reportage in the *Rotherham Advertiser* was also extensive and included particularly upsetting accounts, such as the short passage below, obtained from a surviving unnamed rescue worker 'who had suffered severely' after the second explosion:

> Bodies were discovered reared against the side of a wall, still holding stretchers that a short time ago were ready to be used for others … Three men had been caught by the fall and crushed to death; others presented a ghastly sight; arms and legs were torn off, and in one or two only the torso remained for identification. One man was discovered with the shaft of his pick driven through his body like a sword. In another case a lad was found in a kneeling posture quite dead, but retaining in his hand a whip, whilst the pit pony was disemboweled only a few yards away.

A number of human interest stories were also recounted, including this brief extract concerning the newly bereaved:

> One old lady, over seventy years of age, afforded an illustration of the spirit of resignation, when, in answer to the information that her two sons and a brother were amongst the killed she replied 'It's God's will' and sank sadly to the seat which had been provided for her. The younger women tried hard to emulate the brave example of their elders, but the tragedy was new to them, and it was pitiful to see them weeping for the lost ones covered on the stretchers in the mortuary.

Two contemporary picture postcards under the theme of 'waiting for news', popular souvenirs of the Cadeby disaster. Norman Ellis collection

Inquest, Relief and Inquiry

The inquest formerly opened on Wednesday, 10 July, under the authority of the Doncaster and district coroner, Frank Allen, who knew many of the victims, from mines inspectors to pit lads. Allen swiftly appointed a jury of Conisbrough and Denaby people and took them to the pay station in order to identify as many of the 65 bodies kept there, signing death certificates so as to allowing funerals to take place.

A 'great massed funeral' was expected on Friday, 12 July and 'eight sextents were working hard on a special plot of ground in the Denaby churchyard', according to the *Mexborough & Swinton Times*, with the Archbishop of York leading the service in the parish church. Further arrangements were planned at Conisbrough and, to a lesser extent, Mexborough.

On Tuesday, 16 July, the miners of Cadeby met in the Station Hotel at Conisbrough, in the presence of Herbert Smith, president of the Yorkshire Miners' Association and the Inspection Committee. It was decided that there could be a return to work at the pit as soon as possible, apart from the unsafe South District. Safety and reverence apart, the men and their families just could not afford to remain idle any longer.

Widows of the Cadeby victims eventually received five shillings a week (and one shilling a week for children under the age of fourteen) from the relief fund which had opened for contributions on 11 July. There were 63 widows, aged 18–67, 52 girls and 80 boys, making a total of 195 dependants. By 1929, the number of beneficiaries had reduced to just 19 widows but the committee, despite private and public appeals, found it increasingly difficult to maintain its funds. In March 1936 the balance was only £90 for sixteen widows. A few donations helped but it was the local community who took responsibility to assist the remaining dependants, now aged 48–79. Far more generous provision from public funds

Funeral corteges of several of the Cadeby victims pass through Conisbrough. Norman Ellis collection

A portrait of Sir Richard Redmayne, KCB, taken from his autobiography Men, Mines and Memories. Eyre & Spottiswood Ltd

were provided for the widows of the mines inspectors, Pickering and Hewitt, who got pensions of £150 and £86 a year respectively, along with gratuities of £788 and £479.

The inquest resumed at Conisbrough on 23 July, but there were still fourteen bodies entombed in the mine. The early witnesses were the Cadeby survivors William Humphries, Joseph Farmer, John Bullock and Percy Murgatroyd. In view of a planned public inquiry, Allen advised the jury to limit their verdict to the cause of death which was given as 'accidental death caused by two explosions in the colliery'.

The public inquiry into the Cadeby disaster opened at the Guildhall, Doncaster, on 5 August 1912, chaired by HM Chief Inspector of Mines, RAS Redmayne. Evidence was heard there over three successive days, to 7 August, when there was an adjournment until it was safe for the affected part of the mine to be inspected.

However, it was not until September when the final bodies were recovered from the pit. Distress was especially painful for two widows as their loved ones could not be identified by them. It was feared they may have been 'buried under another name' (*Mexborough and Swinton Times*, 28.9.1912). Frank Allen and the inquest jury assembled again at the colliery offices on 21 September 1912, when Mary Dove explained that she had been unable to identify her missing husband, Willie. There was a similar story from Hannah Stone who was only able to recognize her husband's (Frederick's) boots. All the coroner could say was that the husbands of the two ladies 'were buried somewhere in the parish'. The last burial

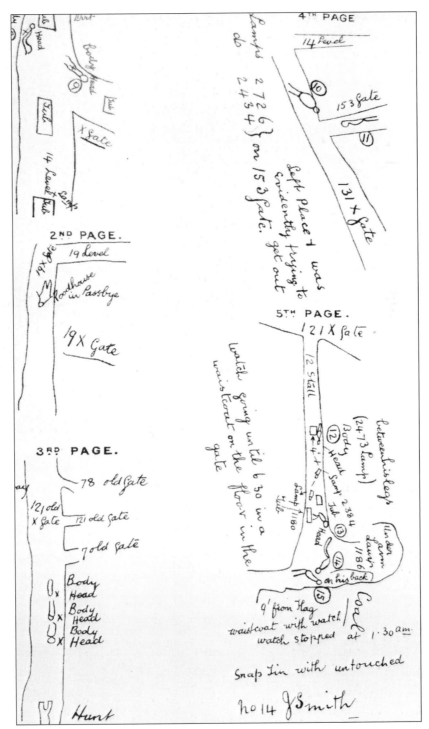

Detail from the notebook carried by Herbert Cusworth, assistant under-manager, who was killed in the second explosion and used in evidence during the official inquiry. Author's collection

service was then held two days later at All Saints', Denaby Main, with the 'supposed widows' Mrs Dove and Mrs Stone present.

Following a partial inspection, on 30 September, the official inquiry resumed on 1 October but the prospect of a full inspection had to be abandoned since the South District was still considered too dangerous for access. Redmayne had to make do with a second-hand report of the workings made by another inspector, wearing breathing apparatus. The last day that evidence was heard was on 5 October.

Redmayne's detailed report was published by the Home Office in 1913. Regarding the first explosion, in his conclusions the Chief Inspector thought that the fire which originated several years earlier had never been fully eradicated, as shown by the explosion of 20 January 1912. The conditions on the night/morning of 8/9 July resulted in a more extended explosion. Redmayne questioned Chambers about allowing men to work in a district near where the fire was located and also said that he believed that Chambers' instruction to effectively seal off the exit of the fire area may not have been carried out fully. The second explosion may have resulted from a large accumulation of gas on the 'rise' side of the district following the first explosion, ignited at the fire until an explosive mixture was formed.

The Chief Inspector paid tribute to the skills and bravery of the rescue teams but found the way in which the rescue operations had been organized at the mine as 'defective'. In particular, Mr HS Witty, agent of the colliery, should have issued instructions prohibiting into the mine all persons not provided with written authorization. A guard should have been placed at the outbye end of the south plane to prevent unauthorized entry, which would have resulted in a far smaller death toll. He was also critical of the management of the colliery allowing persons to risk their lives in order to recover bodies.

The management of the Cadeby and Denaby Company were not in breach of the 1911 Coal Mines Act but many lives would have been saved if, as Redmayne rightly stated, the affected district, an area known to be fiery, had really been properly sealed months earlier – with techniques they used *after* the disaster – but getting coal appears to have been far more a company (ie WH Chambers') priority. The men's safety less so, perhaps. The miners' advocate Herbert Smith had already become famous in connection with rescue work and cross-examination at recent inquiries, for example at the Whitehaven disaster in 1910. Workhouse-born, no one was more aware of the potential poverty and danger that mining families had to endure. Smith's father had been killed in a pit accident before he was born and his mother died shortly afterwards. Adopted by a childless miner who shared his surname, Smith worked as a pit lad from the extremely young age age of ten. Passionate, eloquent and forthright in his representation of the miners during the Cadeby inquiry, Smith harangued WH Chambers about the dangerous working conditions in the affected district. But Chambers, in the words of Jim McFarlane, was 'the king of Denaby…master of his own domain, did not broke any union challenge to his absolute right to manage the pits as he saw fit' – even though he lost close management colleagues and his own nephew, in what became South Yorkshire's worst twentieth-century pit disaster.

Exceptionally, four Edward Medals were awarded for acts of bravery relating to the Cadeby disaster: George Fisher, deputy (1st class); Harry Hulley, deputy (1st class); Walter Henry Prince, contractor (2nd class); and Walter Henry Prince, mechanical engineer (2nd class).

Returning to the memories of Edward Thompson, we should always remember that camaraderie is such among coal miners that to risk life during an emergency was taken for granted, despite rule and regulation:

Now the green grass grows over the graves of these men, some of whom I knew and feel honoured to have known them, for they gave all they had. They tried hard in the first place to deal with a highly dangerous mining condition, only to be beaten when within sight of achievement. In the second place, the most gallant men who went to their rescue knew of the possibility of a second explosion, because all the ingredients were there, but they went in and many paid the penalty with the loss of their lives. It was a meritorious effort by all concerned to the high traditions connected to the mining industry.

In 2004, I interviewed a former Cadeby miner, Eric Crabtree (b.1932), who, as a young gas and dust tester, actually entered the old South Plane, the very seat of the disaster. The names of some of the victims, chalked on iron girders in 1912, were still visible, even old wooden tubs containing coal. It was an eerie and frightening experience when he was left there alone, and one he has never forgot. Eric, who became a mines rescue man, is probably the last person to have visited the stricken area.

Relatively few inquiries after mine disasters have resulted in effective legislation. One positive outcome of Redmayne's (and a report he had earlier made following the 1911 disaster at Jamage pit, Bignall Hill colliery in North Staffordshire), was that the Home Secretary authorised a Departmental Committee (chaired by Redmayne) inquiring into the circumstances in which spontaneous combustion of coal occurs in mines, its causes and means of prevention. Knowledge gained from this was certainly important in more officials understanding and taking appropriate action to eradicate or safely deal with such fires. With Cadeby in mind, another Home Office committee was established to review mine rescue operations. The resultant code of rules remained in force for many years.

Those killed in the first explosion were:

Charles Alderson, 25, dataller
James Beach (or Beech), 44, dataller
Joseph Boycott, aged 67, dataller
Thomas Burns, 48, dataller
Arthur Carroll, 25, dataller
Robert William Chapman, 37, dataller
Thomas Coady, 32, dataller
George Denton, 21, dataller
Willie Dove, 42, dataller
Arthur Dungworth, 24, dataller
Philip George Evans, 48, dataller
C W Fletcher, 29, dataller
John Fletcher, 66, dataller
William Frankland, 43, dataller
W H Godsmark, 28, dataller
William Green, 26, filler
Edward Henderson, 41, collier
George Hindson, 25, dataller

Charles Edward Hunt, 28, dataller
Matthew Jordan, 52, dataller
James McDonagh, 49, collier
John Marrow (alias Marsden), 30, dataller
John Francis Mulhern, 27, collier
Martin Mulrooney, 35, dataller
Percy Edward Nicholson, 18, driver
Charles William Radley, 22, filler
Frederick Richardson, 50, deputy
Cyrus Rodgers, 29, collier
Joseph Roodhouse, 39, dataller & contractor
A E Rowell, 34, dataller
John Smith, 58, collier
George Steadman (alias Young), 31, dataller
James Thompson, 54, dataller
Henry Thompson, 21, filler
Thomas Walsh, 41, dataller

The age range was therefore 18–67, with an average of 36.8, reflecting the relatively mature number of men at work on the night shift. The cause of death of all the above was given as 'burns', apart from Boycott, who died as a result of 'fall and afterdamp'.

Killed in the second explosion:

William Ackroyd, 49, dataller
W Berry, 47, deputy
Robert Peel Bungard (or Bunyard), 21, filler
Charles Bury, 36, manager
James Burdekin, 24, dataller
John William Carlton, 38, deputy
Douglas Chambers, 28, manager
Eli Croxall, 49, afternoon under-manager
Herbert Cusworth, 39, assistant under-manager
William Charles Davis, 26, filler & driver
Robert Neill Eddington, 24, dataller
Sydney Ellis, 32, surveyor
Emrys Evans, 22, mining student
Tom Fleck, 24, dataller
Joseph Benjamin Fox, 24, driver
Arthur Flynn, 21, driver
Richard Gascoyne, 22, driver
Tobias Hancock, 29, onsetter
Michael Hayden, 30, dataller & contractor
George Heptinstall, 28, corporal
Henry Richardson Hewitt, 46, HM Senior Inspector of Mines (Sheffield-based)
Frederick William Horsefall, 21, surveyor
William Humphries, 33, deputy
Samuel Jackson, 32, assistant deputy
Charles Johnson, 33, contractor
John William Kelsall, 26, deputy
William Lambert, 29, dataller
Herbert Neal, 38, onsetter
Jarratt Philips, 44, deputy
William Henry Pickering, 53, HM Divisional Inspector of Mines (Doncaster-based)
Charles Edward Beswich Prince, 23, assistant deputy
Joseph Ross, collier, 37
Samuel Thomas Sanders, 51, dataller
Joseph Shuttleworth, 47, corporal
James Springthorpe jnr, 19, surveyor
Frederick Stones, 34, collier
Thomas Stribley, 35, dataller and contractor
Willie Sumerscales, 37, deputy
Timothy Smith Talbot, 28, filler
John William Tarbrook, 23, contractor
Gilbert Young Tickle, 34, HM Junior Inspector of Mines (WH Pickering's assistant)
Charles Tuffrey, 20, driver
Edmund Jesse Tuffrey, 22, corporal
Joseph Turner, 27, dataller
William Henry Wallace, 56, dataller
Frank Walton, 35, deputy
Benjamin Ward, 30, collier
William David Waters, 31, driver
Samuel Webster, 41, deputy
George Whitton, 32, deputy
Thomas Samuel Williams, 35, deputy
Richard Winpenny, 56, deputy
Tom Wraithmell, 53, onsetter

The age range of the 'rescuers' was understandably less than in the first explosion (19–56 cf 18–67), the average being 33.8, a figure that would be even lower if the experienced deputies, managers and inspectors were excluded. Regarding the causes of death, most of the men (33) were killed in the second explosion by the 'afterdamp'; a further 18 died due to 'shock and injuries'; Prince died from the 'shock of [the] explosion and fall of roof' and Williams' death was attributed to 'burns'.

There were three further unofficial victims of the Cadeby disaster. First, Frank Wood, of Braithwell Street, Denaby Main, committed suicide by drowning himself in the River Don, on Saturday, 13 July. He had lost his brother-in-law in the disaster and was badly affected after assisting in the grim task of searching for and retrieving dead bodies. The second was

James Burns, a member of a five-man Manvers Main rescue team responsible for bringing out bodies on Sunday, 18 August. Burns' mouthpiece was accidentally detached from his breathing apparatus when carrying a body on a stretcher, which meant that he had to inhale some of the poisonous gas pumped into the mine to extinguish fires. His colleagues assisted him to walk 100–200 yards away from the danger area but when climbing over a rock fall his mouthpiece came away again. Lockjaw prevented its replacement and Burns collapsed. After a while his colleagues, assuming the worst, had little option but to make the agonising decision to leave him as their own oxygen supplies were almost depleted. A third additional victim was James Springthorpe, a senior deputy in the affected South district, who gave evidence on the first day of the inquiry, on 5 August, and was said to have had a 'miraculous escape' from the second explosion. Springthorpe died on 25 March 1913, eight months after the disaster but 'from the result of the explosion, 9th July 1912'. Realistically, there were therefore 91 fatalities.

Part Three

Flood and Fire
1913–14

"Then came the rush of water. Mr Bann was just behind me, urging me on and pushing me. The water rose very rapidly, and … the blackdamp, which hung over the water like a thick fog, made it difficult to see where we were going."

Walter Morley, aged fourteen, survivor of the Car House flooding

"Everything for Safety Everywhere."

"PROTO" BREATHING APPARATUS

For rescue and recovery work in mines after explosions, etc.

SMOKE HELMETS

OXYGEN RESUSCITATING APPARATUS

GAS MASKS

GAS ANALYSIS APPARATUS

AND ALL OTHER

SAFETY AND PROTECTIVE APPLIANCES

SIEBE, GORMAN & CO., LTD.,

" NEPTUNE " WORKS, 187, WESTMINSTER BRIDGE ROAD, LAMBETH LONDON, S.E.1.

Telegrams: " Siebe, Lamb, London." Telephone: Hop No. 3401 (2 lines).

'Proto' was one of the twentieth-century brand names used by Siebe Gorman & Company Ltd, who had pioneered the manufacturing of breathing apparatus and diving equipment from their London premises since the early nineteenth century. Their equipment was widely used by mines rescue teams. The Siebe Gorman trade name and manufacturing of safety equipment still exists, in Malaysia.

(5) Car House

Location: Rotherham
Fatalities: 8
Date: Monday, 16 June 1913
Cause: Inrush of water

Another of John Brown's Rotherham area collieries was the scene of a very serious accident, shortly after 8 pm, on a sunny June evening, when an inrush of water from neighbouring Alwarke Main drowned eight (of twelve) men working in the Parkgate seam. The disaster was especially distressing for relatives and friends of the victims – not forgetting the rescue workers – since the recovery of all the bodies proved to be both difficult and lengthy. The last body, that of Charles Palmer, was extracted from the pit 'in an exceedingly advanced state of decomposition' after seven weeks of searching.

Developed in the 1860s, and managed by CWT Fincken ('Finkell' in earlier reports) in 1913, Car House had a good safety record, apparently with no previous serious accidents. The
4 ft 6in Parkgate coal was worked at 410 yards deep (dipping towards Aldwarke). The accident occurred about a thousand yards from the pit bottom where work was well advanced for connecting the two pits. It wasn't an easy task due to the known presence of water in old Aldwarke workings which had to be dealt with by means of carefully placed boreholes and storage areas, complying with the Coal Mines Act of 1911. However, the system failed to protect the narrow heading from a sudden inrush of water.

COLLIERY DISASTER AT ROTHERHAM.

Car House Miners Engulfed By Rushing Water.

EIGHT MEN DROWNED.

Survivors' Terrifying Experiences.

RACE FOR LIFE IN THE DARK.

THRILLING STORIES OF HEROISM.

ENGINE DRIVER'S NOBLE SELF-SACRIFICE.

Dramatic headline from the Rotherham Advertiser. Rotherham Advertiser

On the day before the flooding, a deputy, Albert Moxon, had inspected the heading about 6.30 am and found that one of the bore holes was too large to be plugged or piped, so another was drilled, a few inches away. The colliers were allowed to fill coal and advance the face, additional flank holes also being drilled. The centre hole was extended during the Sunday night and, at 5.30 pm, on Monday evening, another deputy, Sam Lee, came on to the scene. A collier, John Banns, was working with his filler mate, Charles Palmer, both under Lee's safety instructions. During the course of the shift Banns noticed a 'trickling of water', but worked on for a short time and then told deputy Ackroyd about his concern who informed Fincken, the pit's manager. Fincken's response was sensible and realistic: 'Watch the water, and if it increases clear out'. The water did increase slightly but, after hearing an increasingly loud 'clucking noise' the men left the area, initially walking and then running towards the pit bottom, warning and collecting other workers on their way, including the pump lad. George Ackroyd took Banns to the affected district to inspect it when the water burst through the heading. Remarkably, Banns managed to survive the inrush but his mate Palmer, Ackroyd and six others did not. It's hard to imagine the horror they faced.

The Saturday, 21 June edition of the *Rotherham Advertiser* featured news of the disaster on pages 12 and 13 and included a large portrait montage, showing twelve of the 'Victims and Survivors'. Two small images showing relatives 'Waiting for News' were reproduced, courtesy of the *Daily Sketch*, one of several national newspapers who had covered the story earlier.

The all too familiar pit top scene was described in the typical journalistic style of the day:

> The weeping women had congregated in one corner of the yard, and there was none to comfort them in their distress. On the other side stood large groups of men, who discussed critically the chances of rescue being effected. There were many volunteers to join a rescue party but the manager wisely decided (no doubt due to the Cadeby inquiry) not to allow such an attempt, as it would almost certainly have meant a further loss of life. The dismayed watchers … could only wait impatiently until, with light of breaking day, other steps might be decided upon.

The bravery of the late pit deputy, George Ackroyd, was singled out, losing his life after warning others to go to a place of safety. A young engine-driver, John Edward Stacey, was another 'hero' of the disaster, turning back from the pit bottom to warn two other miners but paying the ultimate price for his selfless act. Wilfred Lidster was working with his mate, Rodgers, when they heard Banns shout 'Run for your lives.' Rushing to the pit bottom through rapidly rising water was a 'terrible experience' as was the 'noise of rushing water', for Lidster. But the death of his mate must have been even more upsetting: lagging slightly behind, Rodgers was within a few yards of safety when he was overcome by the water and 'washed away'.

The *Advertiser* also published an eyewitness account from the pump boy, fourteen-year-old Walter Morley and his 'miraculous escape', including the following:

> Then came the rush of water. Mr Bann was just behind me, urging me on and pushing me. The water rose very rapidly, and worse than all, the black damp which hung over the water like a thick fog made it difficult to see where we were going. We had a lamp, and that lighted the way a bit. Mr Ackroyd and Mr Palmer were behind us. I heard

THE CAR HOUSE COLLIERY DISASTE[R]

Photos of Victims and Survivors.

George Ackroyd,
The Deputy who was drowned.

J. E. Stacey,
The Engine Driver, who lost his life through warning others.

Robert Rodgers,
Who was overcome when within three yards of safety.

G. W. Cook,
One of the victims.

Sampson Nightingale,
Who was overcome by the flood.

Peter Nightingale,
His brother, who also lost his life.

Alfred Preston,
Another of the victims.

Mr. C. W. T. Fincken
(The Colliery Manager),
Whose conduct has aroused ge[neral] admiration.

John Bann,
One of the survivors, who heroically saved the life of pump boy Morley.

Walter Morley,
The fourteen-year-old pump boy, whose life was saved by John Bann.

James Murray,
Who owes his escape to the timely warning given by Bann.

Wilfrid Lidster,
Who had a miraculous escap[e]

Oval-shaped portraits of seven of the victims, four survivors and a hero, Mr CWT Fincken, the Car House pit's manager.

them running at first, but when I looked round again I could see no lights, and so I concluded they had been overcome with water.

Six weeks after the disaster, seven of the bodies had been recovered and the inquest, under district coroner Mr J Kenyon Parker, concluded hearing evidence at the West Riding Court, in Rotherham, on Wednesday, 29 July. One of the senior mines inspectors present, Thomas H Mottram, said that it was a mistake by the management of the pit to allow the heading to be driven so near to the Aldwarke dips where there was a known accumulation of water and that a single borehole 'driven from a considerable distance, could have trapped the water entirely without risk to anyone'.

The jury confirmed that each of the seven deaths was due to drowning by an inrush of water from the Aldwarke workings, because the boreholes missed such workings. The jury also found that the system of boreholes was not sufficient and that this was an error of judgement – though not negligence – on the part of the management of the colliery.

Details of the victims were as follows:

George Ackroyd, aged 29, deputy, 14 St John's Road, Rotherham. Married
George William Cooke, 26, miner, 4 Miners' Yard, Greasborough. Married
Charles Palmer, 32, trammer, Primrose Hill, Rotherham. Single
Alfred Preston, 39, trammer, 86 Hardy Street, Thornhill. Married
Peter Nightingale, 21, trammer, 637 Fitzwilliam Road, Rotherham, Single
Sampson Nightingale, 22, trammer, 19 Neville Street, Rotherham. Married
Robert Rodgers, 49, miner, 34 Harpur Street, Rotherham. Married
John Edward Stacey, 22, engine-driver, 67 Kimberworth Park Road, Bradgate. Married

(6) Wharncliffe Silkstone

Location: Pilley, Barnsley
Type: Explosion
Fatalities: 12
Date: Saturday, 30 May 1914

Another colliery widely regarded as a 'safe' pit, suffered a terrible accident, one that might have been far worse if it had occurred an hour earlier. Fortunately the day shift had just about ended, the men either on the surface or at the pit bottom, with only a small workforce getting coal in the affected district.

Wharncliffe Silkstone, named after it's royalty owner, Lord Wharncliffe, was a technologically innovative colliery and provided men for the first mines rescue station in the country, situated at nearby Tankersley. Mr G Blake Walker was the company managing director and the pit was managed by Mr J Wroe. Electric coal-cutters were deployed to 'hole' or undercut several seams, including the 2ft 9in Whinmoor, worked at a depth of 218 yards in the Athersley District, where the accident happened. Most of the coal was filled by hand, conveyed via electrically-driven canvas belt conveyors to No. 2 level and then loaded into tubs.

At about 1 pm there were over 100 miners at work in the Whinmoor workings but when the explosion occurred, forty-five minutes later, a much reduced workforce remained. Preparations were being made to start a coal-cutter. Walter Bailey was running a rope in

Faceworkers working with a Clarke & Stevenson electric coal-cutting machine. George Beedon

front of the machine which a deputy, Lewis Slack, had estimated had about 15–20 yards to cut in the 45 minutes before the end of the shift. At 1.45 pm, after deputy Slack had made his report and when deputy William Clayton was in the box hole, near the pit bottom, the men experienced 'a rush of wind' from the workings; and a reversal of air in the Main Level. Clayton telephoned the under-manager, reporting the news. At the surface the pit engineer, Frank Mairet, who was in the engine house, noticed the automatic circuit breaker trip, indicating a surge of current. Below ground, Clayton was joined by Joseph Sellars, the afternoon deputy who, with Thomas Fearnley and eight others, were about to take a new haulage rope into the workings.

An inspection of the workings revealed obvious signs of an explosion in the No. 2 section. One man, Patrick Maycock, was found slightly injured in the No. 2 level and Thomas Fisher, more seriously injured, was carried out by two men, Harvey and Lang. In total, eleven men who would have been at work kneeling in the low workings were found to be dead, blown over by the explosion and lying on their faces within a short distance of each other. Several were burned, though not badly, and all appeared to have been suffocated by the afterdamp.

A report of the disaster appeared in the Monday edition of *The Times* of 1 June 1914 and included the following:

The under-manager and other officials were in the pit at the time [of the explosion] and news of the disaster was quickly sent to the surface, together with a request for help. Rescue workers were at once assembled. The colliery possesses its own rescue brigade, and sets of special breathing apparatus are kept on the premises. These were taken down, but it was not required to use them. The ventilation was short-circuited, and in a short time the atmosphere was clear enough to allow the rescuers to descend the mine without taking special precautions. The bodies were all brought to the surface and placed in the joiners' shop.

The Times also included a paraphrased account, obtained from one of the men who escaped from the workings, a High Green collier named Patrick Mycock. A similar, but more graphic version, appeared in the *Guardian* on the same day, a remarkable description of what it was like to survive an underground explosion:

When seen at his home his face was terribly burned, and he was suffering from cuts on his head and face. He said that there had been no previous warning of gas and danger, and that the explosion was altogether unexpected. About a score of men were working in the Wynmoor [sic] seam, the general body of colliers having fortunately cleared out about two hours before. The men remaining were engaged in boring a byway, and all went well with the work for a time. It was found necessary to consult the deputy upon a certain matter and he (Mycock) went away to find him. He had only left the working place a few seconds, when he heard a noise 'like a mighty wind in a great gale'. He was immediately thrown off his feet and carried at least ten yards along the main way. He was badly stunned, but he did not lose consciousness. He saw a great flame rush past him, and felt the fire on his face. His clothes caught fire, and he put the flames out, and as soon as the roar had ceased he struggled to his feet … all the men who were working with him were killed.

This Warner Gothard multi-view disaster postcard shows eleven of the twelve victims of the explosion at Wharncliffe Silkstone Colliery. Author's collection

On hearing the news, in the late afternoon, mines inspectors HM Hudspeth and TH Mottram (see below, Maltby Main disaster), left their Doncaster office and managed to reach the pit by 6 pm, by means of motor cycles The bodies had already been brought to the surface when they arrived but an underground inspection soon took place.

It was found that a Clarke-Stevenson coal-cutter had its starter switch on the 'on' position at the time of the explosion, and the switch cover was protected by just one bolt (instead of six); and was therefore not air-tight. It was also ascertained that at the time of the explosion the ventilation fan had stopped for about fifteen minutes to allow it to change over from gas to steam. Experiments showed that when such a stoppage occurred, gas would accumulate quickly near the coalface.

The inquest into the deaths of the victims of the Wharncliffe Silkstone disaster opened at the Miners' Institute, Hoyland Common, on 1 June 1914, presided over by the district coroner, PP Maitland. After the death of John Fisher it was adjourned until 30 June. There were further meetings and adjournments until the conclusion, on 13 August, when the following verdict was announced:

The twelve men lost their lives by an explosion of coal gas on 30 May 1914, by the stoppage and restarting of the fan with a defective coal-cutting machine running at the face causing ignition, and the jury are of an opinion the whole of the management have been very negligent, but not criminally so. The jury trust that the Home Office will give instructions so that the management may be more careful in future.

An inquiry, headed by Samuel Pope, Barrister-at-Law and Thomas H Mottram, HM Inspector of Mines for Yorkshire and North Midland Division, resulted in a report published on 11 November 1914, confirming the inquest verdict. It was, of course, right and proper that the management of Wharncliffe Silkstone were officially censored, though none were named in the final verdict. But even the most impartial of observers could not help but see that officials and the company had got off very lightly – 'just be careful in future' – for what after all was a very serious breach of the Coal Mines Act of 1911. Little solace or sense of justice indeed for the bereaved, their families and several hundred Wharncliffe miners.

Those killed on 30 May were:

George Bailey, 53, machineman, married (5 grown-up childen), of Dick's Croft, Hoyland
Walter Bailey, 19, machineman's assistant (son of above), of Dick's Croft, Hoyland
John Fearnley, 23, ripper/stoneman, married (no family), of 9 Hay Green, Birdwell
William Fisher, 32, collier/filler, married (3 children), of 2 Corwell Place, High Green
Harry James Gardner, 40, labourer at the back of the cutter, married (7 children), of Potter Hill, High Green
Harry Littlewood, 27, ripper/stoneman, married (3 children), of Robin Lane, Mortomley
Arthur Norman, 27, machineman, married (3 children)
Joseph Siddall, 18, machineman/conveyor belt remover, single, of 57 Fitzwilliam Street, Hoyland Common
Fred Walker, 20, machineman/conveyor belt remover, single
John William Wordsworth, aged 24, trammer, single, of 62 Chapel Street, Hoyland Common
Oscar Wood, 24, conveyor belt remover, single, of Potter Hill, High Green

Died later (10 June 1914):

John Thomas Fisher, 40, collier, married (3 children), of Bell's Yard, Hoyland Common

Not long after the Wharncliffe Silkstone tragedy, on 14 October 1914, the Universal pit at Senghenydd, in south Wales, exploded yet again, resulting in a terrible death toll of 439 men and boys. It remains Britain's worst mine disaster.

Ten years were to pass, including the period of the Great War, in which thousands of South Yorkshire miners served, before the next colliery disaster, in a picturesque woodland setting at the edge of Maltby, close to Sandbeck Park, the seat of the Earl of Scarbrough, seven miles east of Rotherham. Only two years earlier, in the aftermath of the 1921 strike, Maltby miners had been reduced to the ignominy of having to walk to the pit to find out if a shift was working or not – and it was often a case of 'not'.

The Wharncliffe Silkstone banner (No.1 NUM Yorkshire Area). Norman Ellis collection

Part Four

The Grim 1920s

"A sound came from the gate [underground roadway] *like a strong wind. I saw a kind of flash and down I went...I put one hand over my mouth and down and kept opening and shutting my nostrils, bending close to the ground to get oxygen, until my legs gave way... and said, 'Its all over.'"*

Arthur Bagley, deputy, a survivor of the Maltby disaster

(7) Maltby Main

Location: Maltby, Rotherham
Type: Explosion
Fatalities: 27
Date: Saturday, 28 July 1923

Maltby Main was a large modern pit, sunk by the Maltby Main Colliery Company (owned by the Sheepbridge Coal and Iron Company) on the concealed coalfield in 1908–11. Two 20ft diameter shafts (downcast and upcast) provided access to the famous Barnsley bed of coal, at a depth of 820 yards. The seam was high quality but also very gassy and, as at Cadeby, was liable to spontaneous combustion. Mr WBM Jackson was managing director and the day-to-day management was in the hands of Mr EH Butler and Basil H Pickering (son of Mr WH Pickering, the much respected mines inspector who lost his life in the second explosion at Cadeby) and an under-manager, Mr M Gabbitas. There were 2,689 men employed, 2,214 of them working underground. Most of the miners lived about a mile away, in the Model Village, a planned estate, commissioned by the colliery company, the work of a local builder, Herbert Mollekin.

Testing for Gas. NUM

Deputies in the pit bottom at Maltby Colliery in the 1920s. NUM

In the months and weeks before the explosion occurred, miners, officials and management were involved in dealing with what clearly was a potentially very dangerous underground situation. The report of the Chief Inspector of Mines, Sir Thomas Mottram, CBE, provides us with a compelling account of the prelude to the disaster, as summarised below:

26 April:	'gob stink' was detected and reported in the 60s airway but the placing of 'dirt packs' appeared to have solved the problem.
7 May:	gob stink was discovered once again, at 52s and 102s.
17 May:	smoke was found in the 60s. The manager, along with an overman, had to have assistance to leave the pit after five hours, seriously overcome from the effects of the gas.
20 May:	smoke discovered from the 60s crossgate and, although further remedial work was carried out, the fire was not extinguished.
22 May:	smoke continues, relays of men try to stem it by ramming sand into crevices, in conditions where 2 percent firedamp was present.
23 May:	the manager returned to work, an underground inspection took place, including miners' representatives and a programme of further safety measures began.
28 May:	the manager found evidence of heat in the 60s crossgate, an old wooden chock was on fire.

2 July: fire breaks out 'round a chock', outbye side of 25s; a workman, while emptying a bucket of stone dust on to the fire, experienced a small explosion which 'blew him out of the hole'.

13 July: the manager reported a 'heavy weighting' of the roof of 52s, fracturing an air pipe, smoke emanating from the pipe; and a 'tremendous fall of roof' occurred during stopping preparations. Several men, including the manager, became unconscious, suffering from carbon monoxide poisoning and had to be helped out to get fresh air.

16/17 July: an explosion of firedamp took place, damaging the upper part of stoppings but the air was clear by 10 pm; but, very worryingly, another explosion occurred resulting in all the men being withdrawn from the pit. Mining engineers countered the manager's orders to continue flooding the affected workings.

18 July: evidence of a third explosion was found and a fourth was felt by a party of explorers.

22/23 July: following an inspection and meeting by officials, miners' representatives and the HM Inspector of Mines it was decided that a volunteer workforce was required to stop off the affected area. Herbert Smith, of the Yorkshire Miners' Association, held a meeting with the men. At midnight, 46 men and officials reported to work, to begin what would certainly be very dangerous remedial work.

Detailed guidance was issued by the colliery agent, Basil H Pickering, to deal with the fire, including the use of inert gas and the building of new stoppings. The latter would only take place following the 'drawing off' of a road accessed via 21s level, the men using breathing apparatus in the process.

On the morning of Saturday, 28 July 122 brave men had descended the mine between 6–6.30 am at the start of the day shift. At 9.15 am a violent explosion occurred in the Low East area, about a mile from the pit bottom, where men were at work at or near the stoppings. They had no chance of survival. The blast brought down massive falls of roof which blocked the approach roads, making access impossible for any immediate or short-term rescue. Only the body of one man, badly burnt, that of the unusually-named Original ('Reg') Renshaw, a roadlayer and one of the oldest of the victims, was recovered, found in 95s crossgate, 130 yards from the East Main Plane. Despite the overwhelming task, teams of rescue teams did their very best to make progress, in the presence of deadly gas and extremely hot conditions (further explosions were subsequently detected). Bearing in mind the tragic experiences

PIT EXPLOSIONS.

27 MEN KILLED IN YORKSHIRE.

SEQUEL TO GOB FIRES.

(From Our Special Correspondent.)

MALTBY, July 29.

This village, one of the largest centres of development in the new South Yorkshire coalfield, is the scene of a disaster only less in extent than that which occurred eleven years ago at the neighbouring Cadeby Main.

Twenty-seven men have lost their lives

Headline from The Times *newspaper, 30 July 1923. The* Times

at Cadeby, new rescue procedures, and horrendous underground conditions, it was decided that the safest way forward was not to access the danger area; and to seal it off by the building of very substantial stoppings, a considerable job which was nevertheless achieved.

With the disaster occurring on a Saturday, local newspaper editors had almost a week to prepare their front pages but reporters were on the scene quickly, their copy also made use of by the nationals. The Monday edition of *The Times* (30 July 1923) printed two full columns on the disaster 'from our special correspondent', the 'pit explosions' described as a 'sequel to gob fires'. For the benefit of readers, a useful explanation of the latter was given:

> Gob fires are smouldering outbreaks in the heaps of debris with which the gob holes, or worked-out places in the coal seam, are filled. They are extremely difficult to quench, and, of course, extremely dangerous in fiery mines such as those of the Barnsley Thick Seam.

The report also described the rush of the emergency services to the pit top, from all directions:

> … rescue parties, doctors, ministers of religion, and ambulance units were rapidly in motion towards Maltby, but only the services of rescue parties could be made use of. These came with oxygen apparatus, vessels containing liquid air, and other appliances from a number of collieries, including Rotherham, Dinnington, Maltby (two), Doncaster, Bullcroft, Denaby, Cadeby, Thurcroft, Brodsworth, Yorkshire Main, Brierley, and Hickleton Main.

Similar reports appeared in the *Guardian* and in the more popular dailies. Locally, the *Rotherham Advertiser* had extensive coverage over several weeks.

The inquest on the body of Original Renshaw was held before Frank Allen, the West Riding coroner, when it was formerly announced that Renshaw had been accidentally killed by an explosion at Maltby Main, on 28 July 1923. His funeral, symbolic for the 26 other victims, was held at a packed Church of Ascension in the Model Village, on 3 August, conducted by the Bishop of Sheffield, with 'a great crowd outside', according to press reports.

Among the surviving oral reports of the disaster day and its aftermath, either published or recorded, is testimony from Arthur Daniels, who was described as 'now over 90' in Reverend Auckland's, *The Growth of a Township*, printed in 1989, when the author was Vicar of Maltby. Daniels, who worked in the tally office, says this about the pit top scene when he arrived there on the Saturday:

> As I approached the pit head for duty at the tally office in the morning I was confronted by a crowd including St John's Ambulance ladies, womenfolk, and also men from other collieries. It all showed the deep affection and solidarity of the well-trained personnel in mining. Many bitter tears were shed by wives and relatives who mingled in the great crowd.

The official inquiry into the Maltby disaster was opened by HM Chief Inspector of Mines, Sir Thomas H Mottram, at Sheffield Town Hall, on Tuesday 18 September. Mottram had succeeded Redmayne as chief inspector and, as we have seen, previously served as the

Herbert Smith (1862–1938), President of the Miners' Federation of Great Britain. NUM

Divisional Inspector for Yorkshire and Midland area, officiating at the Car House and Wharncliffe Silkstone inquiries. Many years earlier, when he was a Tamworth colliery manager, he was awarded the Albert Medal for bravery at the Baddersley explosion (Warwickshire), and in 1910 got the medal of the Bolton Humane Society for his services after the Hulton Colliery disaster. His other responsibilities included membership of the Safety in Mines Research Board and chairmanship of the Mines Department Rescue Regulations Committee. The indefatigable Herbert Smith represented the Yorkshire Miners' Association.

The proceedings were lengthy, occupying seven days, involving 31 witnesses, and over 10,000 questions. From the outset, Smith demonstrated his cross-examination skills, grilling a Maltby deputy (Maurice Sturdy) about the wisdom of allowing men to work when there were gas readings of 4 per cent and more. When the inquiry met on 21 September, Smith was critical during his questioning of Basil Pickering, in view of the fact that thousands of timber props were abandoned in old workings, therefore potential fire hazards. Smith also expressed concern that so many men had been allowed down the pit, despite the obvious dangers. There was compelling evidence from a deputy, Arthur Bagley, who had found as much as 6 per cent of gas in the air in the 95s stoppings. He felt the explosion when helping to erect a brattice sheet at 83 crossgate:

A sound came from the gate like a strong wind. I saw a kind of flash and down I went. Immediately it passed me I rose and tried to get a breath of fresh air, but it was like fire. I put one hand over my mouth and kept opening and shutting my nostrils, bending close to the ground to try to get oxygen, until my legs gave way and I dropped on my side and said, 'It's all over.'

Bagley managed to crawl to relative safety, reaching several men, one of whom telephoned the surface.

The inquiry closed on Thursday, 27 September. It was clear that the disaster was a consequence of an explosion of firedamp from spontaneous combustion in the Low East District of the mine. Also evident, was that the men working on the stoppings did so in conditions where gas was present in the air; but it was not known if the overman, John Stoker (who was killed), took any steps to withdraw the men. Sir Thomas concluded by acknowledging the bravery of the officials of the mine and the rescue brigades.

Sir Thomas Mottram's report was published on 25 February 1924. He concluded that the colliery officials, from the general manager to the deputies, were under the impression that since they were fighting a gob fire they had discretionary power and were not bound by Section 67 of the Coal Mines Act regarding danger from inflammable gas. He stated that the true significance of Section 67 of the Act required a legal ruling but felt that, even if the operations were not infringing the section, they were certainly against its spirit. A legal test case ensued.

Despite the tragedy, it was a great relief to hundreds of hard up families who relied so much on wages from the colliery, that work resumed on 8 September, over five weeks after the disaster. Although Renshaw's body was the only one recovered, later another individual, said to have ginger hair, was eerily glimpsed through a small glass insert. When, eventually, the barrier was safely removed, only ashes remained.

A stained glass window was placed in the Church of Ascension to commemorate the disaster. On Sunday 1 June 2008, during the weekend when Maltby Colliery (now owned by Hargreaves Services plc) celebrated its centenery, in St Bartholomew's church, young people laid 27 individual white roses on the altar, in memory of the disaster victims. Afterwards, Maltby Miners' Welfare Band led a procession to Grange Lane Cemetery for a short service at the grave of the unknown miner. Those who died were:

Bertie Beardshall, 29, collier
Joseph Best, 19, filler
Harold Bourne, 25, haulage hand
Raymond Clinton Bourne, 18, haulage hand
George Brierley, 34, collier
Richard John Brooks, 24, collier
Ernest Clixby, 26, analyst/research chemist
Aaron Daniel(s), 46, collier
Richard Ernest Dunn, 28, collier
William Emberton, 27, collier
Alfred Leslie Fellows, 15, haulage hand
John Henry Garratty, 38, corporal
John William Green, 38, byeworker

George Hickling, 47, ripper
Benjamin Jones, 26, collier
Leonard Meredith, 22, collier
Edward Mitchell, 23, byeworker
Harry Norwood, 30, deputy
George Perrins, 37, deputy
William Preece, 24, collier
Original 'Reg' Renshaw, 48, roadlayer
James Smith, 37, collier
Albert Smithson, 28, collier
Joseph Spibey, 29, collier
John Chandler Spilsbury, 33, collier
John Stoker, aged 30, overman
Sylvanus Turner, 27, collier

Thus, they were mostly younger, fitter miners who were killed, the average age being 29.9; but three of them were still in their teens and of these, Alfred Fellows was only fifteen years old. It was only in 1923, the year of this disaster, that lads of fourteen were not allowed to work underground. Ernest Clixby was particularly unfortunate since he was on loan from the nearby Dinnington colliery, as the Maltby mine company did not have its own chemist. He came from Darnall, Sheffield.

After Maltby, a series of smaller, but very different disasters, continued to remind everyone involved in the coalmining industry, from the government and its mines inspectors to managers, officials and workmen, that there was no need for complacency in regard to safety, both above and below ground, at South Yorkshire pits.

(8) Nunnery Colliery

Location: Sheffield
Type: Paddy mail
Fatalities: 7
Date: Monday, 3 December 1923

Said to be 'one of the safest pits in the country [by the *Sheffield Daily Telegraph*]', 7 men were killed and about 45 injured (15 of them seriously) in a disaster at the Nunnery Colliery, only a mile or so from the streets of central Sheffield. The accident happened early on the Monday afternoon shift, at 2.15 pm. About 120 men (some early reports say 130–140 passengers) were riding in hauled tubs (the paddy mail), from the shaft bottom to the workings, on an inclined road when the rope snapped, whereupon the convoy shot backwards at a terrific speed over several hundred yards. The men had no chance of jumping clear before the tubs crashed.

The accident occurred in the Main East Plane of the 307 yard deep Silkstone pit, one of two shafts at the colliery, which was owned by the Nunnery Coal Company Limited. The general manager was Mr WH Mascall, who acted as agent, with Mr CS Magee as the certified manager. An under-manager, Mr JT Bradwell, was responsible for the Silkstone workings. Coal and men were routinely wound up a steep (1 in 4 to 1 in 7) incline by a single rope driven by a steam engine at the surface. The men were hauled via the paddy on the same rope at the start and end of each shift, between the East Plane and Hewitt's Level, over a distance of about a mile. The rope was made of steel and one and a half inches thick. This method of transport had existed for six years.

The paddy train comprised 44 tubs, all but two used for man-riding, and as many as four men occupied some of them. The embarking point was opposite the entrance to the First North Level. A man had been injured in the workings and was being carried up the plane on a stretcher but there was insufficient room for the bearers to get by. The paddy train was drawn up a short distance so as to allow the stretcher to pass to the First North Level.

The mail attendant, Colin Chappell, then ordered the men who had taken their seats to disembark from the tubs. He communicated with the engineman by means of a series of audible signals, each number indicating a particular action. Chapell signaled a '5', which meant the engineman drawing up steadily; and then he signalled '1', to stop the train. Consequently, after a slow haul of about 40 yards, the train stopped and about 120 men embarked.

Chappell then signalled '8' to let the engineman know that everyone had boarded and then a '4' for the train to be slowly lowered down the incline. After 40 yards of travel, at about 3 mph, the train suddenly began to gather speed. A haulage man standing nearby,

Harry Scott, shouted to Chappell (who was not aware of the speeding up) to signal the engineman for the train to be slowed, which he did by placing a flat knife across the overhead wires. Walter Stockton, the engineman, and his assistant, Walter Proctor, subsequently stated that they had received a signal, '1' (to stop), in place of '4' (lower steadily) which Chappell had tried to send. Procter pulled over the reversing lever and the engine stopped but they noticed that the rope was slack. It had broke and the load had gone. The runaway train gathered tremendous speed down the incline, crashing at Cain's Junction, 377 yards from the starting point, several of the tubs jumping the rails. There was widespread carnage, some men clearly killed and many others maimed, injured and badly shocked.

The rush to the colliery and the pit top was described in the next day's edition of the *Sheffield Daily Telegraph,* who had a reporter on duty 'a few moments after the disaster'. Approaching the scene 'over a rough road', he described it as 'a veritable sea of mud, scores of anxious women, children and men … hastening towards the Nunnery pit'. He continued:

They met stern-faced men coming from the place and held them to inquire the extend of the disaster and if any of their friends were involved. The hardy pit workers, with that magnificent calmness, which almost characterises their conduct in the face of disaster, maintained a solid bearing … And … the crowd pressed on and on until the approaches to the pit were reached.

SHEFFIELD PIT DISASTER.

Seven Men Killed In Runaway Train At Nunnery Colliery.

FIFTEEN SERIOUSLY HURT

Thirty-one Other Casualties: The Scenes At The Mine Head.

How the Sheffield Daily Telegraph *featured the Nunnery Colliery paddy mail accident.* Sheffield Daily Telegraph

Around the colliery offices … was a scene of energetic excitement on the part of the men who were straining every nerve to cope with the situation. Telephone bells were ringing all over the place, and grave-faced men ran hither and thither, each one on some mission bent, but all displaying an alacrity to be at the post of duty when the great call of danger to their comrades had arisen.

Testimony from 'another lucky survivor', Edward Shaw, of Duke Street, 'who described his experiences to our representative whilst calmly smoking a cigarette', was recounted as follows:

I was in a tub when the rope broke, and immediately we began to run back. The speed was terrific … I should say we went down about half a mile in less than half a minute … after the crash … I scrambled and fought my way through the wreckage as best I could, but it was terrible in the dark, and hearing the screams and the moans of my mates.

The Times and other newspapers included quotes from several disaster eyewitnesses, including 'a young miner', Thomas W Jackson, of Park:

We boarded the tubs of the paddy train as usual and set off along the incline on the main road. We were moving nicely when suddenly I felt the rope smash. I was in darkness, as all our lamps had been jolted out. The train ran away at a terrific speed. I knew the tubs would buckle up like matchwood when they struck anything … the next thing I knew I was thrown clean out … and thrown heavily on the track. I found afterwards that the tub was wrecked in two. Men all around were moaning and were unable to stand up. I dragged myself clear of the wreckage and lay down until help came.

The *Sheffield Daily Telegraph* continued coverage of the disaster in its 5 December edition, under the headlines: HEROES ALL and STUNNING STORIES OF THE NUNNERY DISASTER. This included a report below, with the subhead the 'Dying Man's Cheers' (from John Turner who died shortly afterwards, and who also lost his son):

He had been in one of the tubs which was so badly smashed that pieces had to be sawn out in order that he might be liberated. The screams and groans were terrible to hear but Turner grinned cheerily whilst the cutting away operation was in progress. He had an idea that one of his legs which had been instantly amputated…could be replaced; but above all you had to admire the way he was cheering the others on. Yet as soon as he was placed on the stretcher for removal to the base he died.

In its 10 December edition, the *Sheffield Daily Telegraph* reported on the 'remarkable scenes' at the funeral of many of the victims at the City Road Cemetery, when,

… the strains of the *Dead March* reached the ears of this vast crowd of people, both women and strong miners alike were reduced to tears. An elderly man, whose cheeks were wet with tears, was heard to remark, 'It is only by a miracle that my two sons are not being buried with them today!'

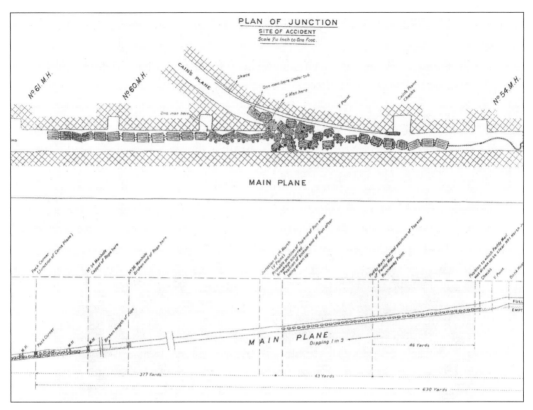

A plan used at the official inquiry into the Nunnery Colliery accident. Author's collection

A 'Shilling Fund' was established in the hope of raising sufficient cash for the widows and orphans, started with a contribution of one thousand shillings by the *Sheffield Daily Telegraph*.

The official inquiry into the Nunnery colliery disaster opened in the city's Council Chambers on 7 May and lasted two days, with seventeen witnesses called. Herbert Smith once again represented the miners. The Chief Inspector of Mines, Sir Thomas Mottram's report to Emanuel Shinwell MP, Labour's Secretary for Mines, was published on 11 August by which time Mottram had retired. The conclusions and recommendations included the following:

> The disaster was caused through the breakage of a part of the haulage rope which had been in use for nineteen months ... I do not wish to attach blame to the management in respect of the broken rope.
>
> I am not satisfied that all the examinations of the haulage rope were as thorough as they might have been, nor do I consider that the weekly statutory reports made by appointed persons always complied strictly with the requirements of Section 66 of the Coal Mines Act 1911 ...
>
> I am of the opinion that the provisions of Section 66 of the Coal Mines Act 1911 should be amplified so as to require a daily examination of machinery, gear and other appliances of the mine used for hauling persons below ground ...

The splicing of ropes used for hauling persons on inclined planes should not be allowed.

The maximum life of [paddy haulage] ropes ... should be limited to eighteen months.

Details of those who died, all from Sheffield, were as follows:

William Thomas Birch, aged 53, married, 14 Rubens Street, Park: died 'from injuries to the body'
Charles Bowden, 62, collier, married, 14 Rotherham Street: died 'from a fractured skull'
Charles Needham, 60, collier, Bernard Street, Park: died 'from a fractured neck'
Bernard Newton, 18, driver, Princess Street: 'injuries to the head and body'
Thomas Walter Turner, 21, fitter, single, 36 Harrogate Road (cause of death not given)
John Henry Turner, 49, collier, married (father of the above), 30 Harrogate Road: 'had fractured both legs'
Charles White, 37, collier, married, 69 Thames Road: 'died from a fractured spine'

Almost two generations were to pass before the next major paddy train disaster occurred, at Silverwood Colliery, near Rotherham, in 1966.

(9) Thorne Colliery

Location: Moorends, Thorne, Doncaster
Type: Shaft sinking
Fatalities: 6
Date: Monday, 15 March 1926

Pease and Partners Limited of Darlington began sinking operations here in October 1909 and, during the next seventeen years, must have been increasingly worried about the wisdom of their sinking costs, amounting to £1.5 million (= £45 million today). However, the human cost was immeasurable.

The most easterly pit on the Yorkshire Coalfield, situated eleven miles from Doncaster and barely above sea-level, the creation of two extremely deep shafts of Thorne Colliery spanned the Great War, and was beleaguered with recurrent water problems and technical challenges. The process was hardly complete when disaster struck. Six men plunged to their death down the No 2 shaft when the pit-head engine that controlled the scaffold on which they were working broke down. Described with alliterated headlines in the local press as a 'Mysterious Mishap', it was not the first shaft tragedy at the new pit. Most notably, a sinker was killed and seven others injured, on 13 December 1910, when a pump and its associated equipment fell down the shaft, crashing into scaffolding. Earlier, a man died in one of the shafts as a result of carbon monoxide poisoning during sinking operations; and a man named Van Hoof was killed when he fell out of a hoppit (large man-riding bucket) at a landing stage.

The 1926 accident happened at 12.20 pm, a couple of hours before the sinkers were due to finish their shift. The background to the tragedy is well described in the *Doncaster Gazette* of 19 March 1926:

" In the Midst of Life— "

Tragedy Swift and Sudden at Thorne Pit.

Six Men Hurled to Death by Mysterious Mishap.

Thorne and the new mining village at Moorends have been plunged into mourning this week through a terrible acident which occurred at Thorne Colliery on Monday, when six workers who were applying the finishing touches to No. 2 shaft were plunged to their death through the scaffold engine at the pithead breaking.

The victims were:

Edmund Thorley (33), first chargeman, married, Durham Avenue, Thorne.
John Hansbury (34), second chargeman, married, of Killaturley, Ireland, lodging in Middleton's Yard, Thorne.
John William Barley (51), sinker, married, Lower Kenyon Street, Thorne.
Charles Henry Walton (33), married, Durham Avenue, Thorne.
Ernest Clark (26), sinker, single, Field Side, Thorne.
John A. Reed, single, living with his grandmother in Durham Avenue, Thorne.

The headlines in the Doncaster Gazette *focused on the uncertainty of working life and death by 'a mysterious mishap'.* Doncaster Gazette

They were working on a portable scaffold suspended by a wire rope from the capstan [a revolving cylinder with a vertical axis used for winding a rope or cable] engine and they were 80 to 90 yards from the pit bottom, which is 963 yards deep. Suddenly the scaffold collapsed, and the men were hurled into water which would be six to eleven feet deep. The supporting ropes from the capstan, about 1,000 yards in length, ran off the drums and down the shaft. Scaffolding ropes and everything that might have caused an obstruction crashed down the pit shaft and fell on top of them.

The *Gazette's* intrepid reporter was allowed to see inside the building ('a shed') in which the drums were housed, courtesy of the pit's manager, Mr G French and noticed the broken bearings. About 100 tons of material were said to be covering the men, making the recovery of the bodies very difficult. Major HM Hudspeth, now the Deputy Chief Inspector of Mines, arrived at the pit on the afternoon of the disaster.

Nationally, *The Times* covered the disaster in its 16 March edition and included this comment, based on an interview with the colliery's agent, Mr CF Hoyle:

… the engine suddenly cracked up in an inexplicable manner, with the result that the ropes ran off the drums down the shaft. He [Hyde] was on the scene immediately afterwards and was lowered in the hoppit, but all that he could see was a few pieces of wood floating on top of the water.

The inquest was held at Thorne under the Doncaster District Coroner, Mr F Allen, who stated that though 'failure of the human element' was a possibility, there could be no suggestion of 'serious blame' being attached to any person. One of the witnesses was George Carter, the foreman sinker who, fortuitously, had left the scaffold at 9.50 am, after inspecting the work. He said that there had never been any problems in lowering and raising the scaffold. Another key witness was George Barley, the banksman, who admitted that the scaffold was moved without any signal having been given to him. Two labourers and the capstan engine driver, Alfred Ingham, also gave evidence, the latter saying that there had never been any previous problems in raising or lowering the scaffold. He described how the engine started as normal when there was 'a sudden jerk'. Three 'possible theories' were put forward by engineers as to the possible cause of the disaster, but, after a fifteen minute retirement, the jury returned a verdict of 'accidental death', adding that there was no evidence to prove whether the accident was due to mechanical failure or human error.

The report of the official inquiry, chaired by Major Henry Moore Hudspeth, was presented to Parliament on 30 March 1926, and understandably included a good deal of technical information, particularly in relation to the pawls (pivoted levers whose free ends engaged with a cog wheel or ratchet so that they can only turn or move one way), drums and bearings, all associated with the capstan. Durham-born Hudspeth, aged 40, was also the new Chief Mining Engineer and member of the Safety in Mines Research Board. He concluded that the pawls were so fitted that in the event of the engine being driven against them, the disaster would result. He recommended that pawls should not be fitted of worm-driven capstan engines unless they could be arranged so that they could avoid this. All this was of little or no consolation to the families of the bereaved who would have received very modest financial compensation.

Shaft sinkers were an extreme form of mineworker who travelled from pit to pit and area to area, bringing with them a high level of skills – and bravado – so necessary for such a difficult and hazardous job. They often resided in temporary, 'frontier-like' buildings or in

TWO OF THE VICTIMS.

E. THORLEY.   E. CLARK.

Two victims of the Thorne pit-sinking accident: Edmund Thorley and Ernest Clark. Doncaster Gazette

lodgings, while work was in progress, though some did settle down, becoming permanent members of new colliery communities. Even their appearance, usually garbed in oilskins to combat mud and water, was very distinctive.

Details of the men who died were given as follows (all living at Thorne, several of them being neighbours):

John William Barley, aged 51, sinker, married, Lower Kenyon Street
Ernest Clark, 26, sinker, single, Field Side
John Hansbury, 34, second chargeman, married, of Killaturley, Ireland (lodging in Middleton's Yard
John Allen Reed, 21, sinker, single, living with his grandmother, Durham Avenue
Edmund Thorley, 33, first chargeman, married, five children, Durham Avenue
Charles Henry Walton, 33, sinker, married, Durham Avenue

Part Five

Depression, Disasters and Orwell
1930–36

"Farewell Fanny old pet"

Last message from a North Gawber miner,
chalked on a piece of coal.

(10) Wath Main

Location: Wath-upon-Dearne, near Rotherham
Type: Explosion
Fatalities: 7
Date: Monday, 24 February 1930

A large audience of miners attended a Safety in Mines lecture in Wombwell, two days after seven men were killed in an explosion at nearby Wath Main colliery. It was reported that

'the assembly rose as one man, and with bared heads stood bowed in silence ...'
(*Mexborough and Swinton Times*)

The first explosion occurred before 7 pm, towards the end of the afternoon shift, in the Billingley Drift, two miles from the pit bottom. Two men, William Hart and Samuel Walton, were working in the affected district when the first of two explosions occurred. Walton was building up the goaf side corner of a pack and Hart was laying rails closeby. Hart's flame lamp was suspended in the inbye side of the prop, next to the goaf. Both men heard a 'bump', followed by a fall of roof into the area. Immediately afterwards, a flash of light was seen, the first of the explosions. Although burnt, Hart managed to help his more seriously injured colleague to a safe a area and informed the afternoon deputy, John Russell, of the situation. Shortly afterwards, when men in adjacent areas were being told to evacuate their work places, another blast was heard, blowing open the doors on 30s level and raising a large cloud of dust.

Evacuation of the pit and rescue work was organised through Mr MC Martyn, the colliery's manager, assisted by under-manager Walter Kelly and various officials. Rescue teams were soon on their way to the Billingley Drift, later joined by the new local mines inspector, Mr EH Fraser. The nearby Wath Joint Rescue Station provided rapid assistance, one of its leaders being its assistant instructor John Poole who continued searching 'stoically' after coming across his own son. John Poole junior, along with Ernest Cusworth and John King were found dead. The *Rotherham Advertiser* of Saturday 1 March included a brief quote from the brave rescue man:

It was a terrible sight to see these dead men. They were unrecognisable. My son had gone 250 yards towards safety when he was overcome. I supervised the rescue work, and it is an experience I shall never forget. The men were all burned and blackened, and the only way I could identify my son, although he was 6ft 3in in height, was by a pair of new boots he was wearing.

Two others, Allott and Unwin, were got out alive but only survived for a few hours in Montagu Hospital. Two more rescued miners, John Dyson and John Russell, died in the hospital on the Wednesday. One young man, Alfred Lenton, was said to be 'recovering' in the Friday newspaper. Hart and Walton were described as 'still under medical attention' at their homes.

A new pulley wheel being hoisted into place at Wath Main in 1924. Giles Brearley

STORY OF THE WATH COLLIERY

SEVEN MEN KILLED BY EXPLOSION OF GAS.

STARTLING MISHAP IN BILLINGLEY DRIFT.

BEREAVED FATHER'S SPLENDID FORTITUDE

TEN MEN OVERWHELMED.

GALLANT EFFORTS AT RESCUE AND RECOVERY

INQUESTS OPENED

QUESTIONS IN PARLIAMENT.

THE KILLED.

JOHN ALGERNON POOLE.   ERNEST CUSWORTH.   JOHN DYSON.

THOMAS FRANCIS KING.   HERBERT ALLOTT.   LEONARD UNWIN.

INQUEST OPENED.

A Fortnight's Adjournment

THE JURY'S FUNCTIONS

"NOT TO FIND A SCAPEGOAT."

RESCUE HERO.

John Poole, assistant instructor at the Wath Joint Rescue Station.

JOHN POOLE.

RECOVERING.

Spectacular coverage in the Mexborough and Swinton Times *included pictures of the victims.*
Mexborough and Swinton Times

'Eager volunteers' also assisted the rescue process, described as follows in a full-page report in the *Mexborough and Swinton Times*:

> A great number of these were boys, some of whom hurried to the pit in their ordinary clothes, and did not wait to change before going down. These boys proved to be extremely useful for carrying water to the rescue parties as they carried on their trying work.

By midnight and through the early hours – despite a heavy fall of snow – a large crowd had assembled at the pit-head, including anxious women and children. An anxious crowd also waited for news at Roman Terrace where several of the men lived.

The inquest opened at Wath Town Hall on Wednesday, 26 February, with Mr J Kenyon Parker, the Sheffield County Coronor presiding. As usual, Herbert Smith was in attendance, representing the miners. Two mines inspectors, Humphreys and Frazer, were present as was the colliery manager, MC Martyn. The first-day proceedings principally concerned identification and medical evidence, though the coroner took pains to say that it was the role of the inquest to inquire into the circumstances touching each death, and for the jury to decided if the cause of death was due to accident or neglect on the part of workmen or management; and if there was any breach of the 1911 Coal Mines Act. He also said that he did not intend the inquest to be 'a roving inquiry to find a scapegoat', emphasising that coal mining was 'inevitably a dangerous occupation'. After the identification of the first three dead miners, the inquest was adjourned for a fortnight, until 13 March. The resumed inquest included reference to a possible government inquiry and featured testimony from the mine's manager, Michael C Martyn. It appears that a broken flame safety lamp had been found buried in the area where Hart and Walton were working. The coroner's inquiry was eventually concluded, with the following verdict and comments of the jury:

> We find that the seven men lost their lives by burns and shock through an explosion of firedamp in the Wath Main Colliery on 24 February 1930 but there was not sufficient evidence to show how the gas became ignited. We should like to subscribe to the comments made by the coroner on the bravery of the people concerned.

> [*South Yorkshire & Mexborough Times*, 4 April 1930]

An official inquiry, chaired by the new Chief Inspector of Mines, Sir Henry Walker, went ahead, in Wath Town Hall, opening on 22 May. It lasted seven days and Walker's report was present to the Secretary for Mines, Emanuel Shinwell MP, on 1 October. Samuel Walton's broken lamp was suspected as the source of ignition and Walton himself felt sure that it had been damaged when being struck by falling stone from the gob area. The inquiry concluded that this indeed was the cause of the first explosion, the glass of the lamp breaking in the presence of firedamp brought down by the fall in the gob which both Walton and Hart heard. Thus, a freak accident brought about an almost immediate explosion, followed by a second, the outcome of which was the death of seven miners and injuries to three others.

Details of those who died are as follows:

Herbert Allott, 27, 36 White's Buildings, Wath
Ernest Cusworth, 31, miner, 12 Princess Street, West Melton
John Dyson, 37, miner, 42 Stockwell Road, West Melton
Thomas Francis King, 55, miner, 6 Regent Place, Mexborough
John Algernon Pool, 21, trammer, Station House, Station Road, Wath
John Russell, 42, deputy, Wath Road, West Melton
Leonard Unwin, 46, miner, 6 Cawood Street, Mexborough

(11) Bentley Colliery

Location: Bentley, Doncaster
Type: Explosion
Fatalities: 45
Date: Friday, 20 November 1931

Bentley people suffered a great deal during the 1930–32 period. The 1926 general strike and miners' lock-out remained fresh in the memory for many residents and the depression during what one veteran Sheffield miner called the 'wicked Thirties', was beginning to hit

Tommy Henwood (right) laying a wreath at the annual Bentley disaster memorial event, Arksey Cemetery, 2003. The author

hard everywhere. Miners and their families struggled to survive on a reduced income from short-time work. To make matters worse, many of their homes were affected by the Don floods of September 1931; and then, to cap it all, a dreadful disaster occurred on a black Friday evening, in late November.

Every November an open air service is held in Arksey Cemetery, to commemorate the 45 men who lost their lives in the Bentley Colliery disaster of 1931 and also the 7 victims of the 1978 paddy mail accident at the same pit. The 23 November 2003 ceremony was particularly well attended, it being the 25th anniversary of the second disaster. During the course of the commemoration I spoke to many people in the distant hope of contacting anyone present who may have worked at the colliery at the time of the first disaster, 72 years earlier. Fortunately, I was able to meet and subsequently interview Tommy Henwood (b.1911), who was a guest of honour at the memorial, laying a wreath in memory of his former colleagues.

Tommy Henwood had started work at Bentley in about 1924, soon to be employed by his collier father, helping him in the North East District Barnsley seam. He had just finished work on the Friday day shift when news reached him that an explosion had occurred in the evening, so he volunteered to help, assisting his dad. At times speaking very emotionally, this is an edited extract of what Tommy remembered:

I went down and got my pony. I was told to take sand bags, not far from the pit bottom. We got to the district where the explosion was. The air was turned round with the blast, reversed. I was told to go towards it as in a couple of seconds it would go back to normal. We had a right bad time of it. My pony would not go … I told him to go in his own time and all at once he set off and pulled the tubs with the sandbags, taking them to where they were needed and I unloaded … My father told me to take them [the bodies] to the pit bottom, and to hurry back with more sandbags. He was doing some running about. I told him I was running about and he was working me to death. He told me that I would pull through. From the pit bottom the bodies were taken up to the ambulance room … I came out of the pit and went to have a look around and thought that there were one or two blokes I had missed … one bloke was still in the pit … I attended the [service and] funerals in Arksey Cemetery. I had to come out of the church the first time. It was too much for me.

Some years earlier, in 1997, I was able to meet Doris Kitching, who was born in Bentley in 1920, so would have been a girl of eleven when the disaster occurred. Her father, Thomas Hopkinson, was a Bentley miner and keen member of the local St John's Ambulance group. 'Tommy the Ambulance Man' always carried a first aid box during his shift, in case he needed to administer medical help to any workmates. That was certainly required on the evening of the disaster but his unselfish assistance also resulted in family tragedy. Here are Doris' childhood memories of the sad November evening day and its aftermath:

Dad was at work on his afternoon shift. Granddad and I were playing Ludo … Suddenly granddad looked up and listened, there was the sound of pit boots on the

road, I think it was about 6.30 pm … there had been an explosion at the pit. He left me with a neighbour and went to the pit yard … the street was filled with fearful people who were anxious to gain news of loved ones or friends. Mum and grandmother rushed home after hearing the news whilst shopping. As the men were brought out dead she scanned each one anxiously, each name chalked up on a board. Dad was the last to be brought out, badly hurt. He had insisted on staying behind to give first aid … Dad just managed to say a few words, he asked about me and died a few hours later … The whole village was in mourning. All the coffins were placed side by side in St Philips' church and most were buried together in Arksey Cemetery … our house bore such grief and sadness and I was bewildered by it all … many miners who survived the disaster never worked underground again, it

Thomas Hopkinson, who was awarded a posthumous bravery award. Doris Kitching

Medal and certificate awarded to the widow of Thomas Hopkinson by the workers' newspaper, the Daily Herald. *Doris Kitching*

ORDER *of* INDUSTRIAL HEROISM

INSTITUTED BY
The Daily Herald
Presented as a mark of respect and admiration to T. HOPKINSON. a brave man who in a moment of peril thought more of others than of himself

date 3ʳᵈ Janʸ 1932.

shocked them so much. The piano stood still and silent in our front room … no laughter, no singing … I cried a lot when he died but when I went to bed I looked through the window at the moon and felt happy because I thought I saw Dad's face and it made me feel safe and happy.

Thomas Hopkinson was posthumously awarded the Order of Industrial Heroism by the *Daily Herald*, and his widow was presented with a commemorative medal and silk ribbon in honour of his bravery.

Mrs D Smith, writing to me in 2006, also recalled her childhood memories of the disaster:

I can just remember men standing on the corners, not speaking, and a paper boy shouting something about a special edition of the paper … there were a lot of children left without fathers … An uncle of mine got killed, leaving a widow and seven children.

Such stories remain, of course, very valuable, providing testimony unavailable from contemporary printed sources. That's why John Woodhead's book, *The Bentley Pit Disaster*, remains so useful, since it contains interviews with local people affected by the disaster, recorded back in 1975.

As expected, many columns of news coverage, as well as compelling photographic images, were soon available locally in the weekly *Doncaster Gazette* and in the *Doncaster Chronicle*. The nationals also reported on the disaster the very next day, Saturday, 21 November, using what facts they could muster from their 'correspondents'. The *Daily Mirror's* headline, on page 3, was SEVENTEEN MINERS KILLED ON BLAZING PIT whilst *The Times* reported the disaster more factually, on page 12, as DONCASTER PIT EXPLOSION, with a sub-head

SEVENTEEN MINERS KILLED IN BLAZING PIT

Fifty Men Trapped Amid Flames and Rush of Gas

27 INJURED

Sheets of Fire and Falls of Roof Hold Up Rescue Parties

Seventeen miners were killed and twenty-seven injured when fire broke out after an explosion last night at Bentley Colliery, near Doncaster.

When the explosion occurred hundreds of men were cut off from the pit bottom by falls of roof in the galleries in which they were working.

The majority of them succeeded in reaching safety, but a party of about fifty were trapped amid flames and a rush of escaping gas.

Sheets of flame and constant falls of roof held up the rescue work, and it was several hours before many of the injured could be brought to the surface.

"PIT SEETHING WITH FLAMES"

Victims' Clothing Burnt Off Their Bodies

The explosion occurred about 7 o'clock, when there were about 1,000 men in the mine.

Hundreds of them were cut off by falls of roof, but with rescue parties quickly on the

Anny Ondra, film star, whose engagement to Max Schmeling, the German holder of the world's heavy-weight championship, is rumoured in Berlin.

BENTLEY MOTORS PURCHASE

Rolls-Royce, Limited, to Produce New Sports Car

The mystery behind the purchase of Bentley Motors, Ltd., by the British Equital's Central Trust, Ltd., is cleared up by the announcement which the *Daily Mirror* is able to make to-day, that this corporation acted on behalf of Rolls-Royce, Limited.

Developments in the negotiations were held up for some time while purchasers were found for seventy chassis included in the Bentley company's assets.

These chassis have been purchased by the Jack Olding and Jack Barclay Syndicate, for which Mr. Rolfe Owen acted. The purchase price was between £70,000 and £80,000.

Now that the chassis can be put in circula-

ANTI-DUMPING DUTIES

First List Last Night— 50 Per Cent. to Pay

LIP STICK BAN

The first order made under the Abnormal Importations (Customs Duties) Act was issued last night, less than nine hours after the Royal Assent had been given to the Act.

The Order will come into force on Wednesday next, November 25.

It is provided that if the Board of Trade are satisfied that articles of any class or description comprised in Class III of the Import and Export List are being imported into the United Kingdom in abnormal quantities it shall be lawful for the Board to charge thereon duties not exceeding 100 per cent. of the value of the articles.

The Board of Trade therefore orders that duties to be charged on articles of the classes and descriptions set out in an attached schedule shall be 50 per cent. of the value of such articles.

The schedule names a large quantity of goods and includes pottery for domestic use, sanitary ware, glazed wall and hearth tiles, domestic glassware, furniture made wholly or mainly of metal.

SILK STOCKINGS

Cutlery, hand tools for carpenters and engineers, wireless sets, loud-speakers, telephone receivers, but not including valves, permanent magnets or batteries.

Electric vacuum cleaners.

Typewriters and parts thereof.

Manufactures wholly or partly of wool.

Stockings and hose, wholly or partly of silk or artificial silk, linen handkerchiefs.

Men's and boy's suits, coats, waistcoats and trousers.

Gloves of all descriptions (other than rubber gloves), material not cut ready for sewing into gloves, and glove linings.

Paper, whether in sheets or rolls or otherwise and whether coated or otherwise treated

The German Ambassador.

GERMAN PLEA FOR HELP

"Unable to Continue Annuity Payments"

The gravity of Germany's financial position was emphasised yesterday in a memorandum presented to the Foreign Office by the German Ambassador, Baron von Neurath.

Application is made in the memorandum for the convocation "without delay" of the Special Advisory Committee under the Young Plan to inquire into Germany's economic and financial position.

The memorandum continues:—

"As early as the beginning of June of this year the German Government had arrived at the conclusion that . . . they would be unable to continue the payment of the annuities of the New Plan.

EXTREME TENSION

"The economic and financial situation of Germany has reached a state of extreme tension. The world has increasingly realised the inner interdependence of the different financial problems caused by the situation and the

The Daily Mirror *reported the Bentley disaster with dramatic headlines.* The Daily Mirror

of 16 DEAD AND MANY INJURED. Reporters and editors had a duty not only to inform their readers but provide lively and interesting copy, especially through human interest stories. The *Gazette's* main themes, in its special edition of Friday 27 November, verged on the spectacular: THE PRICE OF COAL; BENTLEY'S TERRIBLE TOLL IN HUMAN LIVES; MINERS BURNED BEYOND RECOGNITION; and MAGNIFICENT HEROISM OF RESCUE PARTIES. This typical sensational style of journalism does require careful interpretation today. Nevertheless, there are many excellent 'vignettes', both descriptive and based on eyewitness accounts. Here is what the *Gazette* said about the arrival – 'in his pit clothes' – of Herbert Smith, the veteran president of the YMA:

> When Mr Herbert Smith arrived he immediately signified his intention of going down the pit. It was suggested to him that he might not be allowed to do this, and he replied, 'They can't stop me'.

And here is the *Gazette's* description of the moment of explosion and horrific aftermath, based on interviews:

> … men were dashed to the ground, against the sides of the road, and into the tubs and props, many being seriously injured, and a sheet of flame swept the stalls almost simultaneously. Many of the men were burned beyond recognition.

A miner, who was working in a stall next to the one in which the explosion occurred, said that without any warning there was a tremendous flash along the coalface, which threw them all to the ground. When the dust cleared they could see the bodies of the men in the next stall lying on the ground. Many were badly burned, their hair and skin burned off and some had their hair burned off.

It was reported that one man was in so much pain when being carried on a stretcher that he 'broke the straps which bound him' and 'had to be held down … by four men' on the way to the ambulance station.

The *Gazette* also reported news of 'a second explosion', though it was not 'of a very serious nature'.

Bentley was owned by an experienced Nottingham-based concern, Barber, Walker and Company, and had been producing coal, via two shafts, from the Barnsley seam, at 624 yards, since 1908. Housing was soon provided for most of the 3,000 or so mineworkers in either the New Village or in council-owned properties. The fiery seam soon caused problems. Forty fires had occurred and, in 1912 (the year of the terrible spontaneous combustion at Cadeby), Dr IS Haldane, a recent member of the Royal Commission on Coal Mines, was consulted regarding the frequency of 'gob fires'. A mines inspectorate report, dated 31 August 1912, stated that the mine was 'in a highly dangerous' condition. William Fryar, the pit's general manager, along with his senior managers, escaped relatively unscathed from safety accusations made by the Home Office (mines inspectorate) later the same year, following a series of legal hearings. Doncaster collieries were then able to subscribe to the new Doncaster Coal Owners' Committee (Gob Fire Research) and access Haldane's first report on Bentley, published in January 1914. A special unit, known as the Prevention of Gob Fires staff (PGF) was established, all 'heatings' and fires (along with investigations and outcomes) detected by its members and by others having to be recorded. In the meantime, Frier continued to make use of extensive stone dusting. A modern mines rescue station, one of the most advanced in the country, was established at Wheatley, near Doncaster.

What follows is by no means a complete narrative of events, abstracted from a variety of sources, but given the limitations of space, may help us to appreciate both the complexities of the disaster and its immediate aftermath.

At the time of the explosion, about 5.45 pm, 85 men were at work in the North East District (one of 8 similar districts, each with their own ventilation system), including two deputies, Harry Hartley and James Hughes. After finishing his inspection at 5.40 pm 'everything seemed beautiful' or in good order but five minutes later 'there was a regular flash of wind and dust', said Hughes. He warned the pit bottom office of the serious situation and the under-manager, Mr T Cook, was informed. Cook contacted the manager, Mr A Longden, who in turn telephoned the agent, Donald McGregor. Longden sent Cook underground to investigate and contacted the mines rescue service, mines inspectorate, local doctors and Mr WJ Ballam, the local miners' representative. After his descent, Cook found that the shift overman, William Fisher, had already summoned the rescue and ambulance men.

Deputy Hughes came across Dan Maloney, who had been working in 140s, badly burned; and then Arthur Kirkland who, though also badly burned, had managed to lift a tub off the foot of a boy, Thomas Hannon, near the 143s junction. A collier, Horace Windle, who had been working in 143s, was also badly burned. These four men were assisted to the pit bottom and given first aid. One other collier, Harry Roberts, was found by pony driver John

Grim-faced volunteers walk across the pit yard, onlookers in the background. Author's collection

Ward, who took him to the 140s new crossgate junction. Roberts was taken to the pit bottom for first aid by a contractor, George Bailey. Several uninjured men managed to get to relative safety under the direction of Hughes. McGregor arrived on the scene and William Brown, the night shift overman.

Work involving searching for the dead and injured continued until about 11 pm when it was thought that all the bodies had been recovered. On learning that five other men were not accounted for, an attempt to get to them, was without success, due to the intense heat. A third explosion occurred at 1 am, just when the exploring party were trying to get to 141s return from the 140s crossgate. Fires were raging and a decision was made to seal off the NE district in view of the great danger. This was completed by about 2 pm and reinforced over several shifts later.

There are numerous official eyewitness accounts of how miners managed to get out of the pit; and also their experiences during and after the explosion. A gob fire deputy, Harry Hartley, supervising work, felt the ventilation change which 'stirred up a great cloud of dust'. John Ward, the pit pony driver already referred to, at the moment of the blast was standing in 148s gate, twenty yards from the face. He was thrown forward on to his face, his pony just missing him. Ward saw no flames but described the 'choking dust … so thick' he could not see the light of his lamp which was on his belt. Richard Darker, another pony driver, was also blown off his feet on the main haulage road (148s). Beastall and 'ambulance man' Hopkinson, badly burned with a broken thigh, were found by 148s crossgate. Although in great distress, Hopkinson managed to instruct the men how to deal with his

A mines rescue team display their equipment outside the Doncaster Mines Rescue Station. Note the small portable canary cage with its resuscitation facility. Norman Ellis

A terribly sad sight: the mass grave containing more than twenty Bentley miners, interred in Arksey Cemetery. Author's collection

The new Bentley memorial and wreaths from widows, children and friends. Author's collection

thigh. Darker and others continued their work, searching and helping the injured and carrying out bodies.

The inquest opened on 23 November, in the pay office of the colliery, the District Coroner, WH Carlile, presiding, principally for identification of the known victims. It met again on 14 December and, after a short retirement, the jury returned a verdict of 'accidental death' and that the men died from injuries received in the explosion.

The public funeral of 31 of the Bentley victims took place on Wednesday, 25 November, many of the men buried in a large common grave at Arksey Cemetery. The colliery resumed work the following day, after five days' closure. The memorial to the disaster was unveiled on the first anniversary of the disaster.

The 18 December edition of the *Doncaster Chronicle* included a tribute to three 'gallant women', Mrs Elsie Wadsworth, Mrs Elizabeth Homer and Mrs Jones, the 'Florence Nightingales' of the disaster, 'who did heroic work in the ambulance room.'

Details of the 45 men who died – and their dependants – are as follows (addresses are for Bentley unless stated otherwise):

William Agnew, 34, miner, 3 Halmshaw Terrace: widow and one child.
James Edward Allsopp, 27, miner, 36 The Avenue: widow and one child.
Charles Atkinson, 37, miner, 26 Asquith Road: widow and seven children
Albert Edward Barcock, 17, pony driver, single: mother a widow
Henry Beastall, 58, bye-worker, 97 The Avenue: five adult children
George Robert Bentley, 46, miner: widow and one child
John Brett, 37, miner, 25 New Street: widow and six children
William Brocklehurst, 45, miner, 13 Coney Road, Toll Bar: widow and three children
John Brown, miner, I Wainwright Road, Doncaster: single
Stanley Buxton, 28, miner, Ivy Dene, Tilts Lane, Toll Bar: widow and one child
Albert Calladine, 31, miner,17 Winnipeg Road:widow and one child
John Callaghan, 37, miner, 32 Milton Street, Doncaster: three children
Ernest Cawood, 50, bye-worker, 205 Askern Road: 2 adult children
Herbert Cheetham, 30, miner, 31 Victoria Road: single
Thomas Dove, 42, bye-worker, 67 Asquith Road: not given
William Farnsworth, 29, miner, 17 Cromwell Road: widow and 4 children (plus one due)
Joseph William Grain, 35, miner: 23 Hawthorne Grove: widow and 7 children
James Roland Greaves, 35, miner, 12 Balfour Road: 3 children
Thomas Green, 42, miner, 33 Arthur Street: widow and 3 children
Leornard Guy, 34, miner, 90 High Street: a widow
Clifford Hayes, 25, miner, 15 Cross Street: a widow
Alfred Hibbert, 44, miner, 3 New Street: 2 children
Thomas Hopkinson, 33, miner, 35 Daw Lane: widow and one child
Albert Edward Huckerby, 29, miner, The Avenue: single
Leonard Jones, 24, miner, 111 Marsh Gate, Doncaster: widow and one child
Arthur Kirkland, 44, miner, 24 West End Avenue: widow and 3 children
Harold Lawton, 31, miner, 34 Winnipeg Road: widow and one child
Arthur James Leyland, 49, miner, 34 Hall Gate, Doncaster: single
John Llewellyn, 47, miner, 27 Cromwell Road: single with dependant mother
Daniel Malony, 35, miner, Grove Street, Adwick-le-Street: five children
Samuel Mason, 47, miner, 39 The Avenue, widow and 2 children

Wilfred Middleton, 36, miner, 4 Fisher Street: 3 children
John Ernest Peck, 34, miner, Tilts Lane, Toll Bar: 5 children
Richard Thomas Perry, 53, miner, 35 Frank Road: 2 adult children
Joseph Pritchett, 53, miner, 197 The Avenue: 7 children
William Pritchett (brother of Joseph), 47, miner, 17 Balfour Road: 4 children
James Rowe, 56, miner, 15 Coney Road, Toll Bar: a widow
George Singleton, 29, miner, 4 Raymond Road, Doncaster: 2 childrern
Lawrence Oliver Sleath, 27, miner, 20 Hawthorne Grove: a widow
John Hilton Smith, 24, miner, 9 Wheatley Park Road: a widow
Samuel William Templeman, 47, miner, 13 Cross Street: 3 adult children
Henry Womack, 44, miner, 9 Fisher Street: six children
William Ward, 41, miner, 30 Hawthorne Grove: six children
Clifford Willcox, 25, miner, 28 West End Avenue (lodgings): single
Harace Windle, miner, 76 Arcacia Road, Skellow: 4 children

Of the above, 14 were already dead when recovered, 2 died shortly afterwards and 24 died in Doncaster Infirmary. Five bodies (those of Brocklehurst, Dove, Mason, Rowe and JH Smith) had to be abandoned in the sealed off NE workings.

There were more than 150 qualifying dependants. Standard compensation was paid by the Barber, Walker Company: £300 (equivalent to over £10,000) for a widow and £100 (= c.£3,300) for each child under the age of sixteen. The Mansion House Fund had reached £30,000 by Christmas 1931 and £38,000 (= £1.27 million) not long afterwards, a huge total in the context of the deep recession. It provided a weekly pension of fifteen shillings (= £25.7p) for widows and seven shillings and six pence (= £12.53) for each dependant child.

The official inquiry into the causes and circumstances of the Bentley Colliery disaster opened at the Co-operative Hall in Doncaster, on 29 December 1931, Sir Henry Walker, Chief Inspector of Mines, in charge. There were eight days of proceedings and the inspector's report was presented to Isaac Foot MP, the Liberal Secretary for Mines in the National Government, on 18 April 1932. Several theories as to the cause of the explosion were put forward and there was the usual lively cross-examination of managers by Herbert Smith, especially in regard to the PGF system which was by no means working correctly. The sealing off of the NE district meant that any inspection of the area to conclusively find the source and cause of the explosion was not possible. There were also conflicting accounts of the extent and severity of the 'heatings' in key areas in the weeks prior to the explosion. It must have been a great ordeal for ordinary miners to give testimony at such a high profile event. Others may have declined to come forward, feeling that their jobs under threat at a time of short-time working. Sir Henry Walker concluding remarks included the following:

I think the explosion was caused by a gob fire [spontaneous combustion] in either the waste between 41s and 140s old gate …

and:

I would like to put on record my admiration of the conduct of those engaged in the work of recovery, conduct which fully upheld the high traditions of the miner.

It is understandable why so may Bentley people – and miners from neighbouring collieries – felt so bitter about the outcome of the Inquiry. Once again, owners and management had

Richard Darker, whose act of bravery merited the award of an Edward Medal, later exchanged for the George Cross. The author

got off very lightly, even in the context of the comprehensive Coal Mines Act of 1911. The mines inspectorate, principally Edgar Frazer and the Chief Inspector, Sir Henry Walker, did what they could, given their extensive workloads, to investigate and report on the disaster, Frazer's bravery subsequently recognised. The inspectors were experienced and fair minded professionals but their social background was far closer to the owners than the miners. The owners themselves were inevitably driven by commercial and shareholders' pressure which cannot have been helpful when financing both existing and new safety systems, though an effective programme of enlargement of the return airways soon began. But the dichotomy of profit and safety remained in place for another seventeen years, including two major South Yorkshire disasters, at North Gawber and Wharncliffe Woodmoor, until the nationalisation of coal mines by Attlee's reforming Labour government in 1947.

Acts of heroic bravery were outstanding in the aftermath of the disaster and, on 16 February 1933, quite exceptionally, seven men were awarded the Edward Medal in an investiture hosted by the King at Buckingham Palace. They were:

Ernest Allport, deputy
Richard Edward Darker, pony driver and haulage hand
Edgar Hamilton Frazer, HM Inspector of Mines
Oliver Soulsby, collier
Frank Sykes, collier
John Ward, pony driver
Philip William Yates, collier

(12) Cortonwood Colliery

Location: Brampton, near Wombwell, Barnsley
Type: Explosion
Fatalities: 8
Date: Thursday/Friday, 8/9 December 1932

An almost forgotten, certainly overlooked, pit disaster, occurred at Cortonwood Colliery at around midnight on 8/9 December 1932. The explosion was in the machine face of the Silkstone seam, when a group of nine men were involved in, or near, shot-firing operations. Four were killed immediately, including the deputy, 51-year-old Alphonso Allen. Three others died shortly afterwards, leaving one injured survivor, 17-year-old James Edward Moore, of 2 Prospect Terrace, Wombwell. It was said to be the first serious accident since the large, two-shaft pit was sunk in 1873 by the Cortonwood Colliery Company Limited.

The Silkstone seam was developed five years before the accident, in 1927, the downcast (No 1) shaft having been extended to 605 yards in order to allow access. The worked seam was less than 3ft in height, so the men would have little space to move. It appears that during the shot-firing a sheet of flame suddenly went across the face, causing death and fatal injuries

Gilbert Dakin, the artist of this accident scene, was killed with five other miners in 1939. NUM

in an instant. It was highly localised to one spot. A man called Horace Caldwell, working about half a mile away at the time, heard nothing. Another, Oscar Frost, just felt a sudden draught of warm air and a 'bump'; and then went to help with the dead and injured. Fred Jackson, however, at work about a hundred yards from the flash, described how the disaster scene was 'obscured by smoke' and how he 'felt hot air' on his chest. He helped with first aid, saying how difficult the rescue operation was due to the dense smoke and foul air. Another man, Alfred Smith, was one of the first to arrive at the scene and his first impressions were that 'the whole team' had been killed. Smith also helped carry out the bodies on stretchers. Edward Myers, 'one of the first to dash to the rescue', according to the *Daily Express* of 10 December, described how he saw two boys (possibly Scargill and Windle) running towards him, 'their clothes blazing, lighting the passages of the pit'. The report continued:

> As they [the boys] got near him yelling incoherently their clothes dropped off until they were almost naked. He rolled them in stone dust and extinguished the flames.

Cortonwood's managers, Mr R Graham and Mr H Fawcett, were joined at the disaster scene by the divisional mines inspectors, EH Frazer and CW Scott. Herbert Smith, the Yorkshire Miners' Association's president also arrived, as did his knowledgeable colleague, Joseph Jones, who had once worked at the pit. The colliery's rescue team arrived quickly, along with a team from the Tankersley Mines Rescue Station but there was little that could be done. Cortonwood workmen had already recovered the bodies. One of the first outsiders to arrive was Tom Bird, the local YMA branch secretary. He went to the ambulance room where he saw the body of Outram, 'clothed in pit shorts, boots, stockings and knee pads'. A second body, that of Allen, was then brought inside. Both bodies were 'blackened and scorched' from the flash. Tom Bird praised the rescue workers for what they had done in such a short time and also visited the affected face, later describing the devastation:

> Props had been knocked out and there was a considerable amount of charring, but practically no dirt about. In one corner of the face were the Dudleys [metal water containers] and snap tins [lunch boxes] of the men who had been carried out.

Details of those who died were given as follows:

Alphonso Allen, 51, deputy, Cliffe Road, Brampton
John William Eccles, 22, 33 Stokewell Road, Wombwell Main (died later)
Fred Humphries, 21, 55 Pearson's Field, Wombwell (died in hospital)
William Landles, 31, married, 35 Carnely Street, West Melton
Walter Nutter, 28, married, Barnsley Road, Wombwell
Royal Outram, 45, married, Victoria Road, West Melton (left 3 sons and his widow was
    pregnant)
Norman Scargill, 17, 6 Goodyear Crescent, Wombwell (died in hospital)
Albert Edward Windle, 18, 70 Firth Road, Wombwell Main (died in hospital)

The men were said to be well known in their local communities. Landles, originally from South Shields, had been 'singing to the wireless' before leaving for work. Nutter was a noted Wombwell footballer, as was Windle, who played for West Melton Rangers and had worked at Cortonwood since the age of fourteen. Scargill, just seventeen, had only worked at the pit for six weeks. Outram, the first to be brought out of the pit, was a veteran member of the Brampton Church Choir and Victoria Church Choir. Allen was a Methodist teacher at Cortonwood Wesleyan Chapel. Several of the wives and mothers described 'a sort of premonition' of impending danger to their loved ones.

A Cortonwood Disaster Fund was quickly established and within a few days donations amounted to about £200 (worth c.£6,684 today), including one shilling (5p) from 'Just a Mite', of Sheffield and three shillings (15p) from 'Thankful'.

Towards the end of one of the most miserable of recessions, just when the pits were beginning to sell more coal, an explosion occurred, on 22 September 1934, at Gresford Colliery, near Wrexham, in north Wales. There were 266 fatalities, making it one of Britain's worst pit disasters. Then, in South Yorkshire, two major disasters within twelve months devastated neighbouring Barnsley area communities. The autumn and summer of 1935/36 was therefore especially grim for mining families who lived in and around the old villages of Mapplewell and Carlton. The explosions at their respective pits, North Gawber and Wharncliffe Woodmoor, resulted in the deaths of 77 men. In February 1935, one man was killed and a further nine injured at Woolley Colliery (near Darton); and less than three weeks before the North Gawber disaster an explosion killed ten men a few miles away, at South Kirkby colliery, in what is now West Yorkshire. A most unusual accident occurred at Hoyland Silkstone colliery in July 1935 during shaft filling operations. Three men, resting in a brick cabin and having their 'snap', were overcome and badly burned in a surface explosion after gas had escaped from the narrow Lidgett shaft that they were in the process of filling. James Dunning (45), George Nutt (44) and Ernest Wright (55) were conveyed to Sheffield Royal Infirmary where they died the following morning. A Dickensian phrase from another era comes to mind for the 1935/36 period: hard times. So hard, that Yorkshire miners joined the great hunger march to London in November 1936.

The well-known author George Orwell had been in Barnsley in the spring of 1936, in search of material for a forthcoming book, published as *The Road to Wigan Pier* (1937). Some of his comments provoked outrage locally after he deliberately visited some of the worst housing areas, including slum properties in Mapplewell. But his descriptions of the hard and dangerous working conditions in the pits were both graphic and fair, winning praise from far and wide. Here is a typical extract:

> Every miner of long standing that I have talked to had either been in a fairly serious accident himself or had seen some of his mates killed, and in every mining family they tell you tales of fathers, brothers, or uncles killed at work … One miner … described to me how a mate of his, a 'dataller', was buried by a fall of rock. they rushed to him and managed to uncover his head and shoulders so that he could breathe, and he was alive and spoke to them. Then they saw that the roof was coming down again and had to run to save themselves; the 'dataller' was buried a second time. Once again they rushed to him and got his head and shoulders free … Then the roof came down a third time, and this time they could not uncover him for several hours, after which, of course, he was dead.

Rightly, Orwell went on to say that it was the 'every-day dangers' such as roof-falls that were the main causes of death in the mines, rather than the 'great mining disaster', usually of course caused by explosions.

(13) North Gawber

Location: Mapplewell, near Darton, Barnsley
Type: Explosion
Fatalities: 19
Date: Thursday, 12 September 1935

Perhaps the most poignant surviving piece of ephemera in connection with the North Gawber disaster is a postcard showing the 'Farewell Fanny old pet' message chalked on a lump of rock by one of the victims. Owned by the Fountain & Burnley company, North Gawber was one of the oldest collieries in South Yorkshire, situated in the ancient parish of Darton, where coal had been mined from medieval times. Two coal-winding shafts were in operation at the time of the accident, the newest (sunk in 1926 and known as No 3) drawing from the Lidgett seam which was being worked about 1,600 yards (almost a mile) from the pit bottom. The Lidgett, only 2ft 6in thick, was a notoriously gassy bed, so firedamp soon accumulated if the ventilation broke down. The coal was cut by electronically-driven machines during the afternoon shift – brought down by shots fired on the night shift – and filled on to electronic conveyors. Working in this seam, the men would have to be in either a prone position or on their haunches.

An explosion of firedamp occurred in the numbers 3 and 4 South Districts, at about 2.45 pm, shortly after the start of the afternoon shift. Coal that had been previously undercut and brought down was being filled (loaded) on to the conveyor which delivered the coal to an electronically driven gate loader, located near the number 3 South Level, and then emptied into tubs. A shot-firer, Friend Clayton, fired a shot in the No 4 face at about 1.40 pm to assist the ripping of the gate and later fired two more shots in coal near the middle gate of No 3 South Face, after which he experienced 'a sudden rush of wind and dust'. Just before the explosion four young miners, James Crow, Robert Chatterton, Sydney Hunter and George Bowen were working close by in the No 3 South Level. Crow, working at the loader, suddenly saw a flash and was thrown down and then engulfed in smoke. There was no noise but a lot of dust in the air. Hubert Kelly, a youth working nearby, was shouting and two others, collier Walter Riley and pony-driver Claud Ackroyd, had their clothes on fire. Crow was able to describe his efforts to drag the injured men away from the danger area, assisted for a time by Friend Clayton. In the course of this he heard distressing calls from Albert Ibberson, a collier, shouting, 'Save me. My head is burning.'

Sydney Hunter, working near the loader, was knocked down on to his face 'as if something had hit him in the back', but struggled to his feet and also tried to help Kelly, Ackroyd and Riley to get to the middle gate. All three subsequently died in hospital from their injuries.

William Boydell, working at the No 3 South face at the time of the blast, felt 'a gust of wind' which blew him up the face, followed by smoke. Instructed by Friend Clayton, he went to assist the injured.

Published on Saturday, 14 September, just two days after the disaster, the *Barnsley Chronicle* was able to piece together a short narrative of events, including the rescue operations, hurriedly compiled before the Friday copy deadline. It included the following account of the crowded pit top scene:

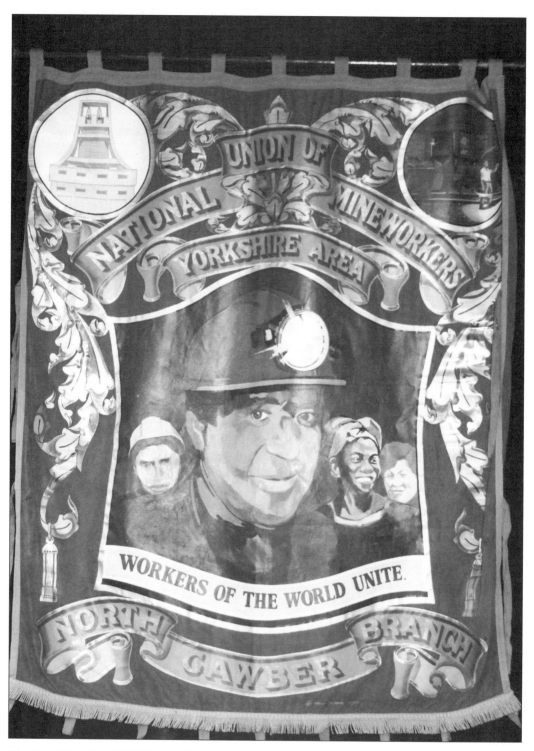

The North Gawber NUM Branch banner. The author

NORTH GAWBER DISASTER INQUEST

Admiration For Doctors, Rescue Parties And Volunteers

DARTON COUNCIL AND BARNSLEY MAYOR OPEN RELIEF FUNDS

NEVER does a mine disaster of any magnitude occur but what is associated with it epics of heroism — stories of men who risk their lives in an endeavour to save their fellow-men or to assuage as much as possible pain and suffering. So it was in the unfortunate calamity at North Gawber Colliery last Thursday. Sorrowing relatives, while lamenting the loss of loved ones, will doubtless find some solace in the knowledge of the supreme courage that was displayed. The hazardous work of rescue called for valour of a high order. Yet, once again in time of peril, in face of death, this trait of gallant fortitude characteristic of the mining community shone through the gloom.

As reported in last week's "Barnsley Chronicle," 15 dead bodies were brought up the shaft and placed in a building in the colliery yard, serving as a temporary mortuary, while the injured were rushed in ambulances to Barnsley Beckett Hospital with all speed.

By Tuesday evening the death roll had increased to 19. George Betton Whewall died late on Thursday night; Hubert Kelly succumbed to his injuries next morning; and the death of Walter Riley followed on Saturday morning. Claude Ackroyd died on Tuesday about 5.30 p.m.

tor of Mines, who was accompanied by officials of the Mines Department, and of the colliery, and by Mr. T. W. Illsley, J.P., of Darfield, representing the Y.M.A. in the absence of Mr. Herbert Smith, President, who was engaged at the South Kirkby Colliery disaster inquest.

ROYAL SYMPATHY

Widespread sympathy was occasioned by the disaster, and on Friday one of the first messages of condolence received was from the King and Queen. It was forwarded from Balmoral to the Earl of Harewood, as Lord Lieutenant of the West Riding, who in turn

How the inquest was reported in the Barnsley Chronicle. Barnsley Chronicle

Imagine a crowd of some 4,000 near relatives, sweethearts and friends surging forward as each tragic party left the pit-head hoping beyond hope, yet afraid that the body which they bore would be that of one of their dear ones. Inside the yard itself were crowds of miners who had so heroically volunteered for rescue work – so many that the best they could do was wait their turn to relieve others who were already engaged in the work. The check office was turned into a temporary dressing room, and on all sides were ambulances with doors ready open to aid those who might be saved.

A rescue man, interviewed by the *Chronicle,* was quoted as saying the following:

It was like hell down there. Everybody is working to get the men, most of whom burned beyond recognition. I have seen some sights in my long experience but never anything to equal those.

Indeed how difficult it must have been, dragging stretchers through dusty and foul smelling workings barely a yard high.

By late evening, the official death toll had reached fifteen, according to the *Barnsley Chronicle's* report. Four men: George Whewall (Thursday night), Hubert Kelly (Friday morning), Walter Riley (Saturday morning) and Claud Ackroyd (Tuesday evening) died in Barnsley Beckett Hospital.

Details of the fatalities were published as follows:

Claud Ackroyd, 20, pony boy, Darton Lane Head, Darton, single
Robert Harold Brant, 53, collier, Four Lane Ends, Mapplewell, married, 2 children
Leo Bunting, 33, panman, caravan, Barugh, married
Jacob Fallis, 43, panman, 99 Honeywell Street, Barnsley, married, 2 children
Richard Hurrell, 27, machineman, 41 James Street, Barnsley, married, 2 children
Albert Edward Ibberson, 53, collier, Allendale Terrace, Mapplewell, married, 1 child
Hubert Kelly, 19, pony boy, Oaks Terrace, Darton, single
Thomas Poyser, 27, collier, Spring Gardens, Mapplewell, single
Walter Riley, 54, collier, 47 Bridge Street, Darton, widower, 7 children
John Thomas Roberts, 40, panman, 52 Wilthorpe Avenue, Barnsley, married, 7 children
James Senior, 46, collier, 7 Woodlands, Darton, married, 2 children
Albert Smith, 39, corporal, 18 Eldon Terrace, Dodworth Road, Barnsley, married

Front-page coverage of the disaster by the Daily Mirror. Daily Mirror

Thomas Marr Smith, 34, borer, High Street, Lane End, Darton, married, 4 children

Clifford Cawthorne Walker, 27, machineman, New Road, Mapplewell, married, 3 children

Joseph Arthur Walley, 44, machineman, Post Office, Higham, married, 2 children

Joseph Stansfield Washington, 36, machineman, 3 Lang Crescent, Burton Grange, married, 1 child

George Whewall, 41, collier, 9 Wright's Terrace, Buckley Street, Barnsley, married, 6 children

John Williams, 28, borer, New Lodge estate, Carlton, single

George Wroe, 35, ripper, 18 Churchfield Avenue, Kexborough, married, 2 children

The disaster featured in most of the Friday national daily newspapers, the *Daily Mirror*, for instance, leading with the front-page headline, SIXTEEN DIE IN PIT EXPLOSION. Its report, which continued on page 3, included a photograph of the pit-top crowd awaiting news. The *Mirror* appears to have had its own reporter there, able to obtain stories from several survivors, including Donald Brook, who had been working on the face, just below where the explosion occurred:

A huge cloud of choking coal dust came down the workings and everything was blacked out. My mates and I searched for our lamps. they were still alight, but in the thick dust they were useless. We groped around and found a crawling man and assisted him to the pit bottom. Then we went back to the danger area, and although the gas made breathing difficult, we reached a number of other men and succeeded in dragging one who was severely injured to safety.

An early visitor to the stricken pit was the veteran miners' representative Herbert Smith, whose son, Harold, worked as under-manager at North Gawber. He was joined by the District mines inspector, Major HJ Humphreys DSO and the Mayor of Barnsley, Alderman Canter.

Among the many tributes and messages of sympathy mentioned in the 21 September edition of the *Barnsley Chronicle* was a brief report concerning the previous Saturday's football match at Oakwell, when both teams (Barnsley and Burnley) wore black armlets and a minute's silence held before the 'bareheaded' crowd. 'Funeral scenes' at Darton churchyard were also reported, concerning the burial of six of the disaster victims, the services conducted by Rev ES Owen, Vicar of Staincross, Rev J Scholefield (his curate), with the Lord Bishop of Wakefield, Dr Seaton, with Canon HE Horne, the Barnsley rector, assisting. There were, of course, similar ceremonies elsewhere, including Staincross, Gawber, Barnsley and Hepworth (Huddersfield). The same edition also included pen-portraits (and a small photographic image) of the disaster victims.

The inquest opened in the West Riding Courthouse, District Coroner Mr CJ Harworth, presiding. His opening remarks paid tribute to the heroism of the rescue workers, volunteers and medical people who worked so hard in the aftermath of the disaster. Numerous stories concerning efforts of miners to help their stricken comrades were recounted in the resumed proceedings, all very distressing for those giving evidence, and of course for families and friends who were either in attendance or able to read about the event later. Particular mention was given to the bravery of Jim Crow, who crawled along the badly affected roadway, dragging two of his badly injured mates to relative safety.

The official inquiry into the North Gawber mine disaster was conducted by Sir Henry Walker, HM Chief Inspector of Mines, at the Town Hall, Barnsley, commencing on 22 October and ending on 2 November 1935. The expert opinion was that the cause was a build-up of gas in an area where ventilation was poor or non-existent, the explosion probably emanating from shot-firing. The inspector acknowledged, however, that absolute proof of the latter was impossible to ascertain but it was most likely the case, based on 'experience and not on speculation'. To fire a shot close to an unventilated place was said to have been a mistake by the firer and the management who failed to appreciate the risk involved.

As usual, dependents were largely reliant on a relief fund, quickly established by Darton UDC and the Mayor of Barnsley. Walter Riley left eight children and, in John Threlkeld's *Pits* book (1985), his daughter recalled that, but for the fund, the family would have 'starved', the older children not having enough money to help.

Part Six

Black August at Carlton
1936

*"The last time I saw my dad was at night before he went to work. We knew he had been killed
…It was very upsetting. I had to go home and tell my mother."*

Sam Owens

Exhausted rescue workers trudge through the mud in the Woodmoor pit yard. Barnsley Chronicle

(14) Wharncliffe Woodmoor 1, 2 & 3

Location: Carlton, Barnsley
Type: Explosion
Fatalities: 58
Date: Thursday, 6 August 1936

Thursday morning was cold, miserable and damp, disappointing for those in Carlton who had booked for a day's club trip to the seaside, but there was always the annual Barnsley Feast Week to look forward to, in a couple of weeks. However, for many families there was little to celebrate when the holiday season started. The disaster at Wharncliffe Woodmoor colliery claimed 58 lives and devastated the local community. It was the last of what we might regard as a major colliery disaster in South Yorkshire, unprecedented in the Barnsley area since Swaithe Main in 1875. Excluding the accumulated deaths of rescue workers as a result of the second explosion at Cadeby in 1912, it remains the worst South Yorkshire mining disaster in modern times.

Sam Owens remembers. The author

Barnsley pit yards soon became muddy on 6 August but the pit top at Wharncliffe Woodmoor colliery was transformed into a quagmire, trampled by thousands of feet as people rushed there from all directions, news having reached them that the village pit had 'blown-up' in the early hours. One elderly Grimethorpe man, told me how he got to know the news, from the bell-man who announced the disaster on a walk around Grimethorpe village. Sam Owens of Smithies, now a sprightly 95 year-old, recalled the moment he got news of the explosion as though it had happened yesterday, when he spoke to me in 2005:

> I was having my breakfast and my mother said, 'What is all this commotion? There are people running up and down the street.' I was told there was a disaster at the pit … She [mother] said get down [there] and see what you can find out. It was throwing it down with rain and I was wet through. Salvation Army was there, giving out cups of tea and Oxo and the pit yard was full of mud … My dad was on the night shift working with a chap called Tommy Smith. After I came home … my Uncle called Williams and I went [back] again to the old Carlton school and waited … until eleven o'clock, probably later. A chap kept coming out [of the school] and reading out names … The last time I saw my dad was at night before he went to work. We knew he had been killed, by word of mouth. It was very upsetting. I had to go home and tell my mother.

Owen Owens, a fifty-six-year-old coal-cutting machine man from Smithies, was one of many incomers to Carlton from north Wales. Owen was identified by his wife, Jane Ellen Owens and was buried in Carlton Cemetery. 'Tommy' (Joseph Thomas) Smith, aged 53, a close neighbour from St Helen's Avenue, a 'packer', died alongside Owen.

Owen Owens. Harry Owens

George Kemp arrived for work after the explosion.
The author

Jack Parkin recalled 'a terrible day for the community'. The author

Thursday was certainly a black day that 85-year-old Carltoner Jack Parkin (aged seventeen in 1936) never forgot. As a young pitlad he recalled asking a passing lady, who was hurriedly pushing a pram, about a WMC club trip to Scarborough, only to be told the bad news. Jack, knowing the potentially dangerous Lidgett seam, rushed to the pit and recalled the scene when he spoke to me in 2004:

> … you could not get into the pit yard. You would think that Barnsley were playing Arsenal, there were so many people there … It was [a] terrible wet day. Parson King [of St John's, Carlton] said it [the bad weather] was in mourning for what happened … [Rev King was] running around comforting people and my old school was used for the bodies … It was a terrible day for this community.

George Kemp, a young lad of fifteen in 1936, employed on the screens where dirt was separated from the coal, arrived at the pit expecting to start work at 6 am. Speaking to me in 2004, he remembered the 'bad morning' quite clearly:

> One of the bosses at the pit top just said, 'Get your checks, just to show you have been here … and go and sit in the engine room ['loco shed']. There were people all over the pit-top, dashing about. I went to the ambulance room where the doctor [Henderson] was … the Union man Eli Sumnall was present. Rescue workers were down the pit … I saw one or two casualties being brought out … We sat … [undercover] as it was cold

and damp outside…until snap time and then about twelve o'clock we were told we could go home…

George had travelled to the pit from his Winn Street home, an old working-class district, known somewhat grimly by most locals as part of Barnsley's 'Barebones' area.

Ron Palmer, also employed at Wharncliffe Woodmoor, was a contemporary and near neighbour of George Kemp but worked underground as a 'box-hole lad', in a cabin near the pit-bottom. Because the deputy found that he could write well, he was given 'office duties', compiling production figures, for instance. Working regular days, Ron was stirred from his slumbers even earlier than usual thanks to a loud banging on his parents' door, a change from the gentle tap of the knocker-up man; and then told to dash to the pit. When he got there, the scene was one of frantic chaos, enough to scare the most experienced and hardened of men. Reporting to a deputy, the seventeen-year-old was instructed to go down one of shafts immediately, despite the fact that he was both frightened and upset by the unfurling pandemonium. When he arrived at his 'office' – and because he could write well – young Ron was issued with a pencil and piece of paper and told to wait by the onsetter in the pit bottom. The teenager's appalling task was to write down the names of all the dead miners as they passed by him, carried on stretchers. The experience haunted him for the rest of his life. Not surprisingly, Ron became a passionate NUM man in his later mining career, at Redbrook (Dodworth) pit.

A twelve-year-old Carlton schoolboy was one of the many early visitors to the disaster scene. Soon to be working as a pitlad at the neighbouring 4 & 5 colliery, Roy Mason became Barnsley's youngest ever MP, holding high office in the Wilson and Callaghan governments of the 1960s and 1970s, most notably as Secretary of State, responsible for Defence and then Northern Ireland. In his autobiography, *Paying the Price*, published in 1999, Lord Mason recalled his impressions of that terrible August morning, thirty-three years earlier:

Even as I rushed to the window to see what was happening, the street outside was full of people, women in shawls, men still buttoning their working togs, all of them with strained, frightening faces. They knew what had happened … My dad and mam were out of the house instantly and I followed behind, with Edna [younger sister] tagging along. There was chaos round the pithead, a harsh glare of lights, crowds milling in despair, women crying, men numb with shock … For hours we watched and waited, desperate for news … Ambulances came, mine safey teams, union representatives, management officials … By dawn, hope was giving way to fear. Rumours swept through the crowd whenever a body was brought to the surface … Wives pushed

Eleanor Bayley was a young nurse who washed the bodies.
Barnsley Chronicle

Nurse Grace Pollendine did what she could to help on the dreadful day. The author

themselves forward, frantic for news of their husbands, brothers and sons. Pit deputies would twitch the blankets covering the dead … the bodies were laid out [in the school] with what reverence could be managed in the hall … There were whole lines of them … I will never forget George and Beryl Formby, two of the very biggest stars of the variety circuit, coming to the Alhambra Theatre in Barnsley to give their services free in aid of the stricken families.

In 1999, it was a pleasure to be able to meet Mrs Grace Pollendine who worked as a nurse at Barnsley Beckett Hospital at the time of the disaster, when an operating theatre was got ready for any of the accident victims. Mr Isaac Rose was the specialist burns surgeon. Grace recalled long hours of duty during the crisis. At about the same time I was also able to meet Walter Caswell, whose father, also named Walter, an experienced and award-winning first aid man, living at 'Long Row', was employed at the neighbouring Woodmoor 4 & 5 colliery. Caswell senior helped with the rescue operations. Speaking in 1987, Eleanor Bayley (nee Caswell), Walter junior's sister and aged nineteen in 1936, was a trainee nurse under Sister Coulson at Beckett Hospital. She was woken by her father at 4 am, who told her, 'Come on lass, there's been an accident at t'top pit.' On arrival, she waited with Dr Hector Henderson, the colliery physician, helping to set up dressings and equipment in impromptu tents and was present when the badly injured Alfred Brown was brought out at 6.30 am. Hours later, she had very grim tasks to perform, working without a break:

Carlton Green School where the bodies were taken. Author's collection

> We had to get down on our knees and, armed with buckets of water, washed the grimy
> burnt and disfigured bodies – it was a pitiful sight that will never leave my memory.

The bodies were laid on clean straw and then taken to the makeshift mortuary at Carlton Green School. In the course of many hours work without a break Eleanor came across her brother-in-law, though did not recognise him until she had helped to wash the dirt away from his face; and then discovered that one of the bodies she was dealing with was of her Sunday school teacher, Herbert Hall; and then there were lads that she recognised from her schooldays in Carlton. How distressing it must have been.

Located less than three miles north of Barnsley, Wharncliffe Woodmoor 1, 2 & 3 colliery (there were actually four shafts, one used for pumping) was also known by the name Old Carlton. It got its modern name from the landowner, the Earl of Wharncliffe, and the Woodmoor seam of coal, first exploited in the 1870s. Run as part of the Wharncliffe Woodmoor Colliery Company Limited, the colliery occupied a large site, with coke ovens, brickworks and an engine shed, placed just south-west of the old village of Carlton, between Carlton Lane and Laithes Lane, employing well over a thousand men and youths. In the 1930s the Company had Sir William and Lady Sutherland of Birthwaite Hall (near Darton) as principal owners/directors, their business interests also including neighbouring North Gawber and Woolley collieries. Sam Diggle was general manager, agent and a director during the 1930s. The pit doctor was Hector Henderson, whose brother, Royston-based Dr James Henderson became a prominent figure during the rescue operations.

The explosion occurred during the latter part of the night shift, at about 3.20 am (according to the shaftman at the surface, who noticed a sudden reversal of air at that time), when men were involved in repair work and making preparations for the day shift. As at North Gawber, it fired in the low (2ft 4in) and gassy Lidgett seam, part of the North East section of the colliery, about a mile from the pit bottom (no 3 shaft). The Lidgett was reached

Edward 4

Daily Heralc

No. 6390   * *   FRIDAY, AUGUST 7, 1936

ALL HOPE FOR 57 PIT VICTIMS ABANDONED

32 BODIES FOUND: GRIM SEARCH GOES ON: ONLY

The dramatic headline on the front page of the Daily Herald. Daily Herald

from above by drifts from the Haigh Moor, and was about 320 yards deep. Lidgett coal was cut by electronically-driven machines, a key focus of the subsequent Inquiry.

The *Barnsley Chronicle* had about twenty-four hours or so to gather first-hand information prior to its copy deadline and the Saturday publication day. It was therefore left to the Friday daily regional and daily national newspapers to provide the most immediate accounts of the disaster. These would have been the reports eagerly read first by local people. A trawl through the British Library's newspaper collection at Colindale, in north London, shows that coverage in the popular press was widespread, usually front-page, content extending into several columns inside; and well illustrated in several examples, the tabloid *Daily Sketch* running a double-page montage of photographs featuring the rescuers, crowd and local doctors (pp. 14–15).

Appropriately, the most graphic and most extensive coverage appeared in the *Daily Herald* (price one penny), then one of the world's best selling newspapers, with over two million daily sales, and very much a 'workers' paper, still part owned by the TUC. ALL HOPE FOR 57 PIT VICTIMS ABANDONED was its front-page headline, under which were two photographs: one of the 'anxious crowd' at the pit top, a few umbrellas evident but most people putting up with the pouring rain; and the other showing grim-faced doctors TF Quigley of Cudworth and Dr J Henderson of Royston. Below the sub-head 32 BODIES FOUND: GRIM SEARCH GOES ON: ONLY ONE MAN SAVED was the main summary report which included the following:

A grim, silent pilgrimage of death, they (the bodies) were taken through a crowd of a thousand at the pithead to a church schoolroom, where 40 nurses from a ten-miles area are helping the doctors. And in that crowd were hundreds of drawn-faced, wide-eyed women. In silence they waited and hoped for their men – who had perished.

It was sensational journalism, evocative of the Edwardian and Victorian eras at its very best (or maybe worst). Readers were even reminded – via a boxed insert within the official list of missing men – that if any of the deceased were 'registered readers' a cheque would be 'sent immediately to their dependants', in other words encouraging more readers to register, a morbid kind of 1930s loyalty card. The main report included reference to the 'amazing luck' of four men who, having finished their work early, had left the pit half an hour before the explosion and there was a piece by HRS Phillpott, extolling the heroism of the rescue workers. News of the disaster continued on to pages 2 and 3, the latter consisting of a spectacular photo montage of the pit-top scene, rescue workers and Reverend Norman King 'offering up prayers for the imprisoned men'. A *Herald* reporter had managed to get a few 'short, bitten-off sentences' from the 'heroic doctor', James Henderson (a Scotsman, who I remember well as a boy when I lived in Carlton):

I am afraid it is hopeless. We have got at the men. A lot of them were killed by violence. Some were smashed and torn up. Others are lying about in attitudes of suffocation, brought about by carbon-monoxide. There is carbon-monoxide all over.

The Woodmoor disaster was featured on the front page of the Mirror, *alongside news about the Spanish Civil War.* Daily Mirror

The immediate aftermath of the disaster was described under a headline on page 2 of SILENT CROWD'S ORDEAL IN RAIN, as follows:

There was a a great half-muffled boom that was heard in Barnsley … The alarm call went round. Doctors, ambulances and rescue parties were summoned. Men and women came out into the darkness and made for the pithead.

One rescue worker was said to have been exhausted, having been at the pit for over five hours, saying, 'The first fall that I came to was about 1,200 yards from the face of the Lidgett seam. There were lots of other falls after the first one.' The report also contained a description of the rescue of Alfred Brown, by engine-driver Joe Brigg, Ted Duerdon 'and two others'. Brown was found 'about 1,800 yards' from the perceived source of the explosion, but was blown off his feet and seriously injured from the after-blast wind.

The disaster did not quite match the front-page coverage of the Spanish Civil War in the *Daily Mirror*, though the report did continue on page 3, and was even able to describe the scene at midnight, when,

… silent crowds were still gathered about the whitewashed schoolroom being used as a mortuary. As the blanket-covered remains were carried in messengers were sent swiftly to the darkened houses of the villages around … Special buses were run all night to take relatives to and from the pit and cars were commandeered to fetch the mothers and wives to the mortuaries … Baskets of food and cans of tea were being handed round the crowd during the night.

Serious reporting mistakes were made. The *Mirror's* correspondent met fourteen-year-old Allen *Cargill* (which should have been spelt 'Scargill') 'in the streets of Carlton', now 'the sole breadwinner for his mother and five brothers and sisters'. Mrs Cargill, '… faced with the arrival of a seventh child in a month or two, sat at home crying silently'. She was quoted as saying: 'I will not believe that he is dead until I see his body myself.' Ernest Scargill's body was not one of the the first thirty-two got out of the pit. He appears to have been one of fourteen fatalities whose injuries were described as 'quite severe' at the inquest, but almost certainly inflicted following carbon monoxide poisoning. Scargill was identified by his brother Norman who lived at 1 Canal Street, Barnsley. Like the *Daily Herald*, the *Mirror* (and its sister publication the *Sunday Pictorial*), took chance to blatantly advertise its own free accident insurance scheme – in case of sudden death – for all 'registered readers'.

The 'quality' national newspapers also included news of the disaster, though in a far less spectacular way. The *Guardian's* report, taken from local journalists, and repeated the first post-disaster edition of the *Barnsley Chronicle*, appeared on page 11 of its Friday edition, even though it had got copy as late as 3 am the same day. It included interviews with rescue workers plus a small map to show the location of Carlton in relation to Barnsley. Quite accurately, it described the 'ice-cold conditions' that the rescue workers and inspectors had to face when they ventured underground, later warmed by blankets and hot water bottles. The report also included reference to the police having to 'rescue' from an angry crowd a photographer who tried to take pictures of the bodies as they were being moved to the mortuary. The *Guardian* published two photographs, one showing the pit-top scene and another of rescue workers on their way to the pit. This newspaper was particular good at

The pit-top scene, captured by an amateur photographer. Ken Eastwood

reporting details relating to the inquest, attempts to get a national day of mourning, and the official Inquiry in the weeks and months after the disaster.

Coverage in Britain's most famous newspaper, *The Times,* consisted of two columns on page 10, under the headline: YORKSHIRE PIT DISASTER. It concluded by saying that operations to recover further bodies was 'suspended at 1 am today' (Friday 7 August), until 6 am, when volunteers would be required for the morning rescue team. It was reported that team members had found that their canaries were affected by gas (five in fact died) during searches and there was 'chaos' approaching the Lidgett face: 'It was just as though a shell had landed in the middle of a dug-out'.

More locally, the *Leeds Mercury* included several quotes from rescue team workers, also repeated elsewhere, but very gruesome copy when published the day after the disaster. William Hogley described the 'ghastly business' of not being able to identify the first man that his team recovered. A similar quote was obtained from Eli Sumnall, who came across two bodies huddled together and 'terribly mutilated' in a disused part of Eight's Face. Sumnall, the local union man, said that he thought the two men were just about to have their breakfast when the blast killed them.

The *Barnsley Chronicle's* narrative of the Woodmoor disaster appeared in its first available edition of Saturday 8 August. Under the headline, HEAVY CASUALTIES IN LOCAL PIT DISASTER was a fairly detailed account of the course of events, compiled the previous day. The opening remarks included reference to the 'courageous volunteers' and 'hardy rescuers':

Details of the 58 victims

Photographs of 51 of the 58 men appeared in the *Barnsley Chronicle* of 15/22 August 1936

Arthur Bird (36), ripper, 14 Oak Street, Barnsley

Henry Birkhead (29), ripper, 3 Wharncliffe Street, Carlton

Lewis Boyd (59), packer, 13 Carlton Road, Smithies

Samuel Brown 14 Martin Road, Burton Grange

Samuel Kirk (28), ripper, 64 Wakefield Road, Barnsley

James William Poole (26), road man, 44 Highstone Road, Worsbro' Common

William Proctor (35), machine man, Newhill Road, Smithies

John Roscoe (41), dataller/labourer, 41 Bedford Terrace, Smithies, Barnsley

William Henry Senior (37), deputy, Burton Bank, Monk Bretton

Herbert Travis (57), packer, 150 Honeywell Street, Barnsley

Archie White (3 ripper, 4 Fernleig Smithies

William Alfred Tomkins (36), packer, 54 Park Road, Worsbrough Bridge

Frank Hadfield (37), electrician, The Durhams, Carlton Road, Smithies

Henry (Harry) Wright (33), ripper, 24 John Edward Street, Barnsley

Joseph Thomas Smith (53), packer, 18 St Helen's Avenue, Smithies

John Brown (31), fitter,159 Upper Sheffield Road, Barnsley, Barnsley

Walter Duerden (29), ripper, Willow Bank, Barnsley

Walter Allott (4 dataller, 15 Pontefract Road, Lundwood

James Robert Miller (40), overman, New Laithes Lane, Carlton

Cecil Chapman (30), haulage, Brookfield Terrace, Carlton

Walter Smith (24), haulage hand, 6 George Square, Barnsley

George Henry Wilson (36), packer, 33 Blucher Street, Barnsley

Ernest Scargill (39), ripper, 1 St Helens Avenue, Smithies

John Bullingham (26), bricklayer, 2 Faith Street, Monk Bretton

Joseph William Harold Abbott (ripper, Willow Ba Barnsley

Portraits of the Woodmoor victims, faithfully assembled by the town's newspaper. Barnsley Chronicle

William Buckley (44), pan man, 7 Lawley Place, Smithies

Frederick Cooper (36), ripper, 111 Sheffield Road, Barnsley

John Fletcher (33), deputy, Langley Terrace, Lundwood

Irvin Foster (35), ripper, New Road, Staincross

Richard Brookes Grimshaw (31), dataller, 56 Smithies Lane, Barnsley

Herbert Hall (55), dataller, Spring Lane, Carlton

Horace Llewellyn Hepworth (33), ripper, Long Croft, Mapplewell

Richard Wright (59), ripper, 7 Grays Road, Carlton

Clarence Parkin (43), machineman, 112 Churchfield Lane, Darton

Victor Clarkson (35), machine man, 50 Birkwood Avenue, Cudworth

Alfred Brown (37)*, haulage hand, 11 Long Row, Smithies

*died in hospital, a single man who lived with his mother.

Ernest Dalby (24), machine man, 51 Priory Road, Lundwood

John Jackson (41), roadman, 27 Bridge Street, Barnsley

Enoch Hulson (59), bricklayer, New Laithes Lane, Carlton

Harold Arthur Lowe (44), dataller, Carlton Road, Smithies

John Henry Waugh (35), packer, 63 Commercial Street, Barnsley

Alexander George Henry Thompson (26), roadman, Fish Dam Lane, Monk Bretton

George Thompson (father of Alexander, 62), road man, 14 Riddings Avenue, Smithies

William Alfred Ellis (21), dataller, 8 Canning Street, Worsbrough Common

Harry Hatfield (30), ripper, 16 Sycamore Street, Barnsley

Owen Owens (56), machine man, 20 St Helen's Avenue, Smithies

Arthur Molyneaux Haigh (26), machine man, 7 Richard Street, Barnsley

John Donelly (36), timber drawer, 7 Park Avenue, New Lodge

Cleasby Bailey (33), timber drawer,6 Wesley Street, Barnsley

William Arthur Bateman (49), ripper, 3 Brookfield Cottages, Carlton

Benjamin Hodgson (36), ripper, 5 Newcliffe Terrace, Cundy Cross

No photograph available

George Farmery (42), deputy, 20 Tempest Avenue, Darfield
James Green (52), ripper, 1 Allendale Road, Darton West
John Edward Henry Hope (34), deputy, 30 Mottram Street, Barnsley
Charles Edward Ismay (32), machine man, Broadway House, Smithies
John David Jones (63), dataller, 5 Newsome Square, Monk Bretton
Henry Lee (39), machine man, 45 St Helen's Avenue, Smithies
William Whiteley (55), dataller, 101 Summer Lane, Barnsley

These hardy rescuers, who strode across the pit yard with sleeves rolled up to the elbows of their brawny arms encountered yet another terror when the got into the workings underground.

The violence of the explosion had shattered the doors controlling the ventilation system and this caused a draught of icy cold air to sweep through the workings with the force of a tornado.

So cold was the air that the first batch of rescuers had to use hot water bottles. Rest, for them was impossible, and in their anxiety to reach their comrades they toiled heroically in the confined space of the Lidgett seam – wrapped in blankets and rugs.

It was the Wharncliffe Woodmoor No 1 team who were the first rescuers to search the affected area, reporting when they surfaced that falls of roof, despite tunneling, had slowed their progress. Broken ventilation doors and the presence of gas made the operation both difficult and hazardous. One of the 'entombed' miners that they were searching for was Bob Miller, an overman and captain of the Carlton rescue team.

The report included a description of 'prayers on the pit hill', conducted by Parson King:

The Vicar … moved among the crowd, stopping here and there to speak a few words of comfort to a stricken relative. When the suspicion gradually began to dawn that there was a heavy death roll the vicar moved to the front of the crowd and offered a prayer for those trapped underground and for the rescue workers, a party of whom were, at that very moment, crossing the yard to the cage. As the Vicar prayed the men bared their heads and stood as if fascinated and apparently oblivious to the the pouring rain.

A miner in pit clothes could be seen practically dragged away by friends. He kept muttering mechanically 'I must go down. I must go go down there.'

The front page of the following week's edition of the *Barnsley Chronicle* (15 August 1936), consisted of a long list of donations to the Disaster Fund, ranging from one shilling from, for example, 'a Liverpool sympathiser', to the £1,000 (c.£37,000 in today's money) given by the Mine Workers' Federation of Great Britain. Within a few days, donations had reached £12,000 (worth c.£444,000 today). Perhaps the most popular celebrity of the day, George Formby, visited the pit and village, and appeared at a sell-out charity concert at Barnsley's Alhambra cinema.

Inside the *Chronicle* special edition, on page 18, under the biblical heading set in gothic type: *Through the Valley of the Shadow of Death,* contained a detailed report on the identification of the bodies, based on the inquest evidence which was opened by the District Coroner, Mr CJ Haworth, at Barnsley's West Riding Courthouse on Friday 7 August, and resumed the following Monday. The medical evidence put forward was that 32 of the 57 cases (excluding Alfred Brown) 'had no burns whatever', 18 had 'extensive' burns and 7 had 'less extensive' burns. However, it was concluded that the 'painless' carbon monoxide poisoning would have meant that all the men had minimal suffering, a statement no doubt appreciated by the already greatly distressed relatives.

Pages 17–19, in a matching typeface, had *Barnsley Mourns with Stricken Families* as the headlines, under which were placed portraits and short obituaries relating to many of the victims. There was also an emotive description of Carlton under the theme of 'Village of Silence' and in particular the Sunday memorial service held in a packed St John's church:

County Borough of Barnsley

Wharncliffe Woodmoor Colliery Disaster

In Memoriam

United

Memorial Service

TOWN HALL, BARNSLEY

at 3 p.m. on

Thursday, August 13th, 1936

conducted by

THE LORD BISHOP OF DERBY

and

REV. F. LUKE WISEMAN, B.A.

(Ex-President, Methodist Church)

assisted by

CANON H. E. HONE (Rector of Barnsley)

Rev. GEO. E. JOHNSON (Mayor's Chaplain)

and the

GRIMETHORPE COLLIERY BAND

" Lest We Forget "

E Cheesman Ltd., Printers, Barnsley.

Programme for the well-attended Memorial Service held in Barnsley. Author's collection

Here was a memorial service conducted by the Vicar of Carlton (Rev Norman King) and among the impressively subdued congregation was the Deputy Mayor of Barnsley (Alderman BF Canter). Dead silence reigned, and relatives found it hard to hold in check the tears, as the Vicar, advancing to the chancel steps, read out the 57 names of the men who had lost their lives – an act of remembrance followed by the solemn tolling of the church bell and the observance of two minutes' silence.

Funeral scenes were also described, particularly at Carlton when Cecil Chapman, Frank Hadfield, Arthur Miller and Ernest Hulson were interred on the Sunday afternoon, 'when a brilliant summer sun beat down on thousands of bared heads reverently bowed'. The Mayor, Councillor Joseph Jones, CBE, JP, himself President of the Miners' Federation of Great Britain, broke down momentarily when reading Psalm 23 and, at the cemetery, a 'white haired women' had to be physically restrained from throwing herself in one of the graves. Thirteen funerals were held on the Monday, at Carlton, Monk Bretton, Cudworth, Darfield and Darton; and an estimated crowd of 4,000 gathered at the entrance to Barnsley Cemetery where Harry Hatfield, Richard Grimshaw, Samuel Brown and Arthur Bird were buried.

Page 11 of the *Chronicle* was dominated by a report on the Civic Service of Remembrance held outside Barnsley Town Hall on the Thursday afternoon, under the headline of 'Miners' Day of Mourning'. However, it's placement was somewhat incongruous, with columns of adverts for 'Feast Week' bus and rail trips, even adverts for dances and used car bargains alongside; but, in all fairness, there was not enough space. A day of national mourning in coalfield areas never materialised, despite great efforts by Joseph Jones and others. But some pits did support the appeal, despite loss of wages, as a matter of comradeship and respect. The Barnsley memorial event was a massive affair, an estimated crowd of 15,000 jamming into the environs of the town's new public edifice. A reporter, mingling with the crowd, had this to say about the occasion:

The crowd assembled a considerable way down Market Hill and along Church Street, and the car park in Lancaster Gate presented a sea of faces. Roofs of surrounding property were used as vantage points, and upon scaffolding surrounding the premises opposite the Town Hall stood workmen, youths, and even women.

On a broad terrace in front of the Town Hall was a group of tragic figures – the relatives of the victims. Widows, mothers, sweethearts and fathers, sat beneath the shadow of the War Memorial and held communion with their lost ones. On the steps below the terrace stood the Grimethorpe Colliery Band whose uniforms presented a contrast to the sombre scene.

As the fingers of the Town Hall clock approached three a hush fell upon the vast concourse and a few seconds before the hour the crowd pressed forward towards the Town Hall ... At the end of the [Armistice Day-style two-minute] silence the siren sounded once more, and a few seconds later thousands of voices were raised in the singing of the hymn *O Love that will not let me go* ... The crowd's demonstration of sympathy concluded with the singing, marked by a deep rugged earnestness, of the hymn *Abide with me*, and as its final cadences died away heads were again bowed and a blessing was invoked by the Bishop.

Perhaps the most symbolic part of the ceremony were the 58 lighted miners' lamps, one for each of the men who died.

The inquest continued into the autumn, with several men giving evidence, saying that they had never noticed any gas in the affected district. The official inquiry, held in Barnsley Town Hall, lasted six days under the chairmanship of the experienced Chief Inspector of Mines, Sir Henry Walker. It was not without controversy. The lead YMA representative was Herbert Smith, now a veteran of 73 mining tragedies. A 'heated exchange' took place on 27 October, between Sir Henry and Joseph 'Joe' Hall, of the YMA. Joe was a brilliant advocate, and was soon to became a worthy successor to Smith. Steeped in the industry, Joe had started working at Darfield Main at the age of twelve. He was determined to make the point that it was dangerous practice for the men to work long hours on a coal cutting machine which he felt was the 'first connection with the accident'; and felt that there was potential danger in the gob area while cutting was in progress. Hall also questioned a deputy, Sam Gallagher, who, under overman Bob Miller's instruction (Miller was killed in the disaster), had fired three shots on the night of the explosion in the main haulage roadway, which was against the Mines Regulation Act.

Crucial evidence that emerged in the published report included the fact that two doors separating the intake airway were found undamaged but 'spragged' wide open. This would

The original memorial to the Woodmoor disaster victims was unveiled by the president of the Yorkshire Area NUM, Arthur Scargill, in 1979. Also present (front, next to Scargill) was the town's MP, and former Carlton miner, Roy (now Lord) Mason. The author

The re-dedication ceremony and establishment of a new memorial site was attended by over a hundred people, including many relatives and descendants, in May 2008. The author

mean that most of the ventilation reaching 1's Level would pass into the main return and little, if any, to 1's face. Discussion also related to the use of stone dust, spread along roadways, theoretically to alleviate the extent of explosions; but it was also combustible material and it was known that 201 tons of limestone had been used during the previous few months. A deputy, Farmery, had been preparing to fire shots but had not done so before the explosion occurred. Also, the cover of the motor of the electronic motor near the inbye end of 1's Level was found on the floor and the cover of the starting switch of the motor was found to be loose. In conclusion, the evidence seemed to point to the explosion being caused by a spark from the switch or the commuter of the loader motor, though there was no absolute proof that this was the case.

In 1979, a commemorative plaque and half pulley wheel memorial was unveiled by the Yorkshire NUM president Arthur Scargill, in what became Athersley Memorial Park. Among the dignitaries was Roy Mason MP (now Lord Mason), who as a boy of twelve years old remembered going to the disaster scene. More recently, a stone frieze representing the Woodmoor miners was sculptured by Harry Malkin and placed near a local health centre. In 2008, the two memorials were combined on a more accessible site, a new plaque and information board was added, marked in a moving ceremony led by the Mayor of Barnsley,

'Lest We Forget': Georgia Ellen Owens Cooksey points to the name of one of her ancestors, listed on the new memorial plaque. The Cooksey family

Councillor Len Picken who, with Councillor Roy Butterfield, had done so much to campaign for and facilitate the new memorial site. More than a hundred people attended, including numerous relatives and descendants, some with Welsh origins. It was a great privilege for me to be involved in the event, and perhaps the most appropriate last word about the disaster is inherent in the work and experiences of children that I had the pleasure of working with at Carlton Primary School.

Details of the 58 victims were as follows:
Joseph William Harold Abbott (32), ripper, Willow Bank, Barnsley
Walter Allott (49), dataller, 15 Pontefract Road, Lundwood
Cleasby Bailey (33), timber drawer, 6 Wesley Street, Barnsley
William Arthur Bateman (49), ripper, 3 Brookfield Cottages, Carlton
Arthur Bird (36), ripper, 14 Oak Street, Barnsley
Henry Birkhead (29), ripper, 3 Wharncliffe Street, Carlton
Lewis Boyd (59), packer, 13 Carlton Road, Smithies
Alfred Brown (37)*, haulage hand, 11 Long Row, Smithies
John Brown (31), fitter, 159 Upper Sheffield Road, Barnsley, Barnsley
Samuel Brown (28), 14 Martin Road, Burton Grange
William Buckley (44), pan man, 7 Cawley Place, Smithies

* died in hospital, a single man who lived with his mother.

John Bullington [or -ham] (26), bricklayer, 2 Faith Street, Monk Bretton
Cecil Chapman (30), haulage, Brookfield Terrace, Carlton
Victor Clarkson (35), machine man, 50 Birkwood Avenue, Cudworth
Frederick Cooper (36), ripper, 111 Sheffield Road, Barnsley
Ernest Dalby (24), machine man, 51 Priory Road, Lundwood
John Donelly (36), timber drawer, 7 Park Avenue, Carlton
Walter Duerden (29), ripper, Willow Bank, Barnsley
William Alfred Ellis (21), dataller, 8 Canning Street, Worsbrough Common
George Farmery (42), deputy, 20 Tempest Avenue, Darfield
John Fletcher (33), deputy, Langley Terrace, Lundwood
Irvin Foster (35), ripper, New Road, Staincross
James Green (52), ripper, 1 Allendale Road, Darton West
Richard Brookes Grimshaw (31), dataller, 56 Smithies Lane, Barnsley
Frank (Francis?) Hadfield (37), electrician, The Durhams, Carlton Road, Smithies
Arthur Molyneaux Haigh (26), machine man, 7 Richard Street, Barnsley
Herbert Hall (55), dataller, Spring Lane, Carlton
Harry Hatfield (30), ripper,16 Sycamore Street, Barnsley
Horace Llewellyn Hepworth (33), ripper, Long Croft, Mapplewell
Benjamin Hodgson (36), ripper, 5 Newcliffe Terrace, Cundy Cross
John Edward Henry Hope (34), deputy, 30 Mottram Street, Barnsley
Enoch Hulson (59), bricklayer, New Laithes Lane, Carlton
Charles Edward Ismay (32), machine man, Broadway House, Smithies
John Jackson (41), roadman, 27 Bridge Street, Barnsley
John David Jones (63), dataller, 5 Newsome Square, Monk Bretton
Samuel Kirk (28), ripper, 64 Wakefield Road, Barnsley
Henry Lee (39), machine man, 45 St Helen's Avenue, Smithies
James Robert Miller (40), overman, New Laithes Lane, Carlton
Owen Owens (56), machine man, 20 St Helen's Avenue, Smithies
Clarence Parkin (43), machineman, 112 Churchfield Lane, Darton
James William Poole (26), road man, 44 Highstone Road, Worsbrough Common
William Proctor (35), machine man, Newhill Road, Smithies
John Roscoe (41), dataller/labourer, 41 Bedford Terrace, Smithies, Barnsley
Harold Arthur Rowe (44), dataller, 9 Carlton Road, Smithies
Ernest Scargill (39), ripper, 1 St Helens Avenue, Smithies
William Henry Senior (37), deputy, Burton Bank, Monk Bretton
Joseph Thomas Smith (53), packer, 18 St Helen's Avenue, Smithies
Walter Smith (24), haulage hand, 6 George Square, Barnsley
Alexander George Henry Thompson (26), roadman, Fish Dam Lane, Monk Bretton
George Thompson (father of Alexander, 62), road man, 14 Riddings Avenue, Smithies
William Alfred Tomkins (36), packer, 54 Park Road, Worsbrough Bridge
Herbert Travis (57), packer, 150 Honeywell Street, Barnsley
John Henry Waugh (35), packer, 63 Commercial Street, Barnsley
Archie White (34), ripper, 4 Fernleigh, Smithies
William Whiteley (55), dataller, 101 Summer Lane, Barnsley
George Henry Wilson (36), packer, 33 Blucher Street, Barnsley
Henry (Harry) Wright (33), ripper, 24 John Edward Street, Barnsley
Richard Wright (29), ripper, 7 Grays Road, Carlton

Part Seven

A Cage Mishap and Five Wartime Disasters
1937–1945

"I was buried up to my neck in sand and dirt but I managed to get hold of the rail and dragged myself clear of the debris. My lamp had been buried but I rushed up the plane and in the dark… I fell down but managed to scramble up again. I am a very lucky man to be alive."

Jack Berry, survivor of the 1942 Barnsley Main disaster

By the late 1930s, the proportion of coal cut by machine had reached 60 per cent, though Britain lagged behind other European coal producers such as Germany where the figure was 97 per cent. Modernisation continued during the Second World War with the introduction of larger, power-loading machines that cut and conveyed coal in a single automated process. Traditional, hand-got methods, however, were by no means eradicated

BARNSLEY MAIN PIT DISASTER
Death Roll 13, with Many Injured and Shocked

HOSPITAL AND RESCUE WORKERS "MAGNIFICENT"

YET another pit disaster has cast its grim shadow over Barnsley, and this time an explosion which occurred on Tuesday at the Barnsley Main Colliery claimed 13 victims.

Those killed were:—

J. A. HARROT, assistant manager, Barnsley Road, Stairfoot.
E. PILKINGTON, under manager, 2, Holly Bank, Victoria Crescent, Barnsley.
G. MARTIN, repairer, 47a, Blenheim Avenue, Barnsley (local Y.M.A. branch secretary).
A. BROWN, filler, 20, Albion Terrace, Tune Street, Barnsley.
W. BURNS, filler, 47, Brinckman Street, Barnsley.
C. WRIGHT, filler, 92, Colley Avenue, Kendray Estate.
V. LOWE, filler, Colley Crescent, Kendray Estate.
W. RUSHFORTH, filler, 54, Birk Avenue, Kendray.
W. LAKIN, overman, 116, Upper Sheffield Road, Barnsley.
R. H LUCK, overman, 89, Park Road, Worsbro' Bridge.
W. HINCHCLIFFE, filler, 6, Rymers Yard, Sheffield Road, Barnsley.
T. COCKING, filler, 62, Milton

appeared more concerned about their workmate's injuries than about themselves." This man remained at the pit bottom until everyone was ordered out of the pit.

One of the stretcher bearers was Charlie Hardcastle, formerly feather weight champion of England and holder of the Lonsdale Belt, who now works at the colliery.

Ever Present Danger

Minor falls and the danger of further explosions caused those in charge of the rescue work to withdraw all men from the pit at one period, but the task was grimly resumed as soon as possible.

As darkness fell anxious relatives flocked to the pit eagerly seeking news of men known to be still in the pit. It was a long vigil however

COUNCILLOR GEO. MARTIN

Coun. George Martin, 47a, Blenheim Ovenue, Barnsley, who was 54, has been Secretary of the Barnsley Main Branch of the Y.M.A. for the past 14 years, and a member of the Barnsley County Borough Council, representing the East Ward, for over seven years. He was Chairman of the Housing Committee and a member of Barnsley Pensions Committee.

The Barnsley Chronicle *headline also featured Councillor George Martin who lost his life in the* Barnsley Main disaster. Barnsley Chronicle

at some pits and at many working faces. Welfare improvements, following years of trade union representation, included paid holidays from 1938. But, prior to state ownership, it was often left to how enlightened a particular mine owner was in regard to the provision of even the most basic of support facilities.

Complicated price lists (piecework rates) often caused wage disputes and ill-feeling between the miners, management and owners; and did not encourage safe practices, or indeed the provision of proper maintenance. Many union officials rightly thought that the wages system actually caused accidents. The whole situation got worse when younger men left the industry for better-paid – and safer – jobs elsewhere, or joined the forces. Coal was in great demand for the war effort but there was a shortage of men at work in the pits and their morale was low, absenteeism doubling. The latter was rarely because of idleness, even at so-called 'sunshine pits' (see the Barnburgh entry, below), but was more due to frustration at the lack of support and sheer exhaustion after rest days were abandoned. A desperate shortage of both coal and miners characterized the 1940s, to some extent alleviated by the introduction of so-called 'Bevin-Boys' towards the end of the war.

In 1935, in the wake of the Gresford disaster, a Royal Commission on Safety in Mines was established, basically to consider whether the health and safety of mineworkers could be improved, in the light of changes in the organisation, methods of work, and equipment since the 1911 Act. Chaired by Evelyn Cecil (Lord Rockley), the Commission's report was published in December 1938. However, due to the outbreak of war, regulation was delayed, until the Mines and Quarries Act of 1954, twenty years after Gresford.

Inevitably, accidents and occasional disasters continued to remind the public of the human cost of coal, though the age of the major disaster, affecting many dozens of fatalities and devastating communities, at least in South Yorkshire, had thankfully waned. However, the war also meant that reportage of fatalities was not given the same extensive treatment in the press and media as before; and the accidents and disasters that did occur, though of course remembered locally for many years, disappeared from general public memory.

One of the first wartime accidents involving multiple casualties (and two fatalities) took place at Sheffield's Nunnery Colliery, on 19 June 1940, when a fall of stone trapped eight men.

What follows (apart from Kilnhurst), therefore, might be regarded as the 'forgotten disasters' of the wartime years.

(15) Kilnhurst (formerly Thrybergh Hall Colliery)

Location: Kilnhurst, Rotherham
Type: Cage winding
Fatalities: 1 (c.17 injured)
Date: Wednesday, 28 July 1937

Almost a year after the Wharncliffe Woodmoor disaster, on 28 July 1937, a serious cage accident occurred at Kilnhurst colliery (known locally as 'Bob's oyle') near Rotherham which could have been a major disaster. The colliery had new proprietors: The Tinsley Park Colliery Company, of Sheffield. The fact that one man was killed and seventeen other miners injured was a bad situation but it could have been far worse. The accident took place at the start of the Wednesday afternoon shift, at 2.45 pm, when a two-decked 'high-speed' cage containing

COLLIERY CAGE MISHAP.

CRASH INTO BOTTOM OF SHAFT.

Men Treated At Rotherham Hospital.

One man was killed and 17 injured when a cage descending the No. 2 shaft of the silkstone seam at the Kilnhurst Colliery on Wednesday, crashed to the bottom of the shaft, which is about 2,000 feet deep.

The men were on their way to work on the afternoon shift, and the cage had completed the greater part of its downward journey when the accident happened, otherwise more men might have been killed.

The man killed was Joseph Sales, aged 54, of 2, Apollo Street, Rawmarsh.

Joe Sayles (who was killed)   **Richard Harper.**

Ten of the 17 injured men were brought to the Rotherham Hospital, along with another man who was injured whilst helping to rescue the men from the wreckage of the cage. Five of the other six men injured in the mishap were taken to the Mexbro' Montagu Hospital.

THE RESCUE WORK.

The task of bringing out the injured from the pit bottom presented difficulty immediately after the accident, in view of the fact that the cages in the shaft in which the accident occurred go down to the Silkstone Seam, and the other shaft of the colliery is only to a much shallower seam. There is a long connecting drift between the two seams, and the problem was whether to wait for repair work to be carried out in the shaft in which the accident occurred, or whether to carry the injured men on stretchers up the long drift. It was decided to await repairs being carried out in the shaft in which the mishap occurred, and about an hour and a half elapsed before the injured could be brought out. This task occupied about three-quarters of an hour.

At the time of the accident Mr. Gawthorpe, H.M. Inspector of Mines, was making a routine inspection in the pit, which belongs to the Tinsley Park Colliery Co., Ltd., of Sheffield.

Shortly after the accident, the manager, Mr. G. H. Willis, and Mr. Herbert Smith, the president of the Yorkshire Mineworkers' Association, went down the pit. The Divisional Inspector of Mines (Major J. Humphrys) and his chief assistant were also among early arrivals at the colliery. The Rector of Rawmarsh (Canon F. G Scovell) and his wife also went to the pit

This factual headline about the Kilnhurst cage accident appeared in the Rotherham Advertiser.
Rotherham Advertiser

eighteen men suddenly picked up speed as it approached the bottom of the 660 yard No 2 (Silkstone) shaft. Twenty-four men in a co-ordinated ascending cage were flung into the headgear at the pit top, but saved from crashing back down the shaft by a safety catch known as a the 'butterfly'. Suffering from 'shock and bruises', this group of men were able to scramble free via ladders and assistance. For all the men concerned, it must have been a terrifying experience, something they would never forget, even after their physical recovery.

Joe Sales ['Sayles' in some reports], aged 54, of 2 Apollo Street, Rawmarsh, riding in the lower deck of the descending cage, was killed, apparently instantly. He left a widow and five children, three of them of school age. Six men: Arthur Spencer, Thomas Riley, Peter Gilgallon, James Gilliver, Charles Pears and Alexander McDonald, were retained in Mexborough Montagu Hospital with leg injuries, several of them described as 'very serious' or 'serious'. Ten others: George Wardingley, Thomas Griffiths, John Griffiths, John Veitch, Albert Barnes, Sam Roddis, John Davis, Edward Gerard, Horace Tuxford, and James Ensor, were taken to Rotherham Hospital. Only two of the latter, Ensor and Gerard, were discharged after treatment. John Wagstaff, assisting in the rescue operations, was also treated for a head injury when struck by an object which fell down the shaft.

Richard 'Dicky' Harper was described as 'hero of the day' in the local press. Travelling on the upper deck, he told reporters that the cage was descending quite normally to begin with, until about 60 feet from the bottom: 'Then something happened to the winding gear, and the cage just dropped. I fell on my hands and knees…and it was this action and the fact that I was near the gate that saved my life or saved me from serious injury' (*South Kirkby, South Elmsall & Hemsworth Times*). His mates were 'huddled in heaps, groaning with pain', Harper saying that Joe Sales lay 'beneath a number of men, and I saw him pulled out'. Harper then attended to the injured. However, in the *Rotherham Advertiser* he was said to have saved himself as he 'leaped into the air' as the cage hit the ground.

Mr T Gawthrop, a Barnsley-based mines inspector, was making a routine visit to the colliery when the accident took place. He was soon joined by the Divisional Inspector, Major HC Humphrys and a Senior Inspector, Mr E Evans, who came from Doncaster. Also on the scene was the miners' union representative, the indefatigable Herbert Smith, probably attending his last serious incident, prior to his own sudden death a year later in his Yorkshire Miners' Association offices in Barnsley (later the Yorkshire and national headquarters of the National Union of Mineworkers).

At the resumed inquest on the death of Sales, the winding engine man, William Henry Hudson, admitted that the 'slow banker' safety device should have been in the place marked 'men' but instead it was on the mark 'coal'. The coroner, Mr J Kenyon Parker, following expert evidence, said that the accident would not have happened if the device had been at the correct mark. The jury brought in a verdict of 'accidental death, owing to an error of judgement on the part of the winder'. It was a courageous and honest piece of testimony from Hudson. Though not excusing the mishap, the winding house itself would have been a hot environment to work in July especially and there may have been distractions from other people in the confined space of the building. Hudson had worked at Kilnhurst Colliery for 42 years and had been engine man since 1924.

One of the survivors, John Veitch, penned a poem 'in memory of the pit cage accident', with the main title of *Perils of the Mine*, though he used the old Thrybergh Hall name of the colliery, which was officially abandoned in 1924. It was not unusual for verses to be composed and printed locally after pit disasters and it is pleasing when such pieces survive, often kept, as this one was, by an affected family.

(16) Kiveton Park

Location: Kiveton, Rotherham
Type: Explosion
Fatalities: 5
Date: Tuesday, 24 June 1941

The colliery worked the Barnsley (401 yards' deep) and High Hazels (313 yards) seams in the early 1940s and the accident occurred in the former seam, which was hand-got. Five men working together received severe burns following an explosion from a gas emission. A pony, though scolded, survived the blast. Word about the disaster soon spread, the local school sending children home. Two of the survivors died after being taken to Sheffield Royal Infirmary: Fred Hoften, aged 67, a deputy and Walter 'Bob' Walker, who was 33. Hoften had worked at the pit for 55 years, starting at the age of twelve, and had been a deputy for more than twenty-five years. William Eames (38) and Jonas Eames (41) died five days later, on 29 June, and Charlie Bedford, the last victim, only eighteen, died on 5 July.

The colliery was owned by the Kiveton Park Coal Company Limited at the time of the accident. A total of 125 deaths of men and boys are recorded in Michael Sampson's book, *A History of a Pit, its village and People* (2007), covering the existence of the colliery from its sinking in 1866 to closure in 1994.

The Kiveton Park wartime accident was not widely reported but this example appeared on the front page of the Worksop Guardian. Worksop Guardian

(17) Bullcroft

Location: Carcroft, Doncaster
Type: Explosion
Fatalities: 6
Date: Friday, 19 October 1941

Bullcroft Main was sunk in 1909–11 and had two shafts to the 684 yard Duncil seam, just after passing through the Barnsley bed at 659 yards. It was the latter bed of coal which was principally worked, a lucrative seam which we have seen was also noted for its potential to 'heatings'. A series of small explosions occurred at a Barnsley face which was subject to spontaneous combustion. An investigating rescue team then faced an explosion in the return airway. The heir to Herbert Smith, miners' leader Joe Hall, present at yet another coalfield emergency, had a narrow escape during the rescue operations.

One man (Baldwin) was rescued alive but died later and two (Buxton and Gyte) were killed outright in the explosion. The other three men were fatally buried under a fall of roof and their bodies were unable to be recovered, the affected District having to be sealed for safety reasons. The Doncaster Amalgamated Collieries Company, of which Bullcroft formed a part, had been formed in 1937 and four years later the owners created a research department in order to investigate issues such as spontaneous combustion.

The men who died were:

A Baldwin, 37, rescue man (died later)
I Buxton, 47, rescue man (not recovered)
I Crane, 39, rescue man (killed in explosion)
William Gyte, 55, rescue man (killed in explosion)
A Orme, 55, rescue man (not recovered)
I Sampson, 42, deputy (not recovered)

(18) Barnsley Main

Location: Barnsley
Type: Two explosions
Fatalities: 13
Date: Monday/Tuesday, 16/17 February 1942

The Barnsley area was rocked again by a mine disaster, on this occasion only two miles or so from the town centre, at Barnsley Main. Two men working in the Fenton seam received serious burns following an explosion of firedamp, one of them dying in hospital two days later. During operations to seal off the dangerous area, by the use of 'stoppings', principally sandbags, a further, and even more violent explosion, took place, resulting in the deaths of twelve more miners/rescue workers. At least thirty other men were either physically injured or suffered from shock as a result of the second explosion. Such experiences, of course, affected miners and their families for many years afterwards. Sealing potentially hazardous workings was by no means uncommon and was regarded as a safe procedure, though the

Reg Batterham, seen here in 2009, was a young miner working with Walter Lodge when the first explosion took place. The author

second explosion in similar circumstances at Cadeby in 1912 was not too distant a memory, particularly for the YMA.

From 1932 (and until nationalisation, in 1947), Barnsley Main colliery was owned by Barrow Barnsley Main Collieries Ltd. The coal was worked via the company's two neighbouring collieries, Barrow and Monk Bretton. The colliery lay within the County Borough of Barnsley, a couple of miles south-east of the town. Its distinctive spoil heap or 'Barnsley's mountain' dominated the skyline. Part of the the Hoyle Mill side of the pit was the site of the old Oaks Colliery, which in 1866 was the scene of what now remains as England's worst mine disaster, when 361 men and boys were killed (and about a hundred bodies never recovered : see volume 1).

On the Monday night of 16 February an explosion and fire broke out in the Fenton seam, at about 7.30 pm, which resulted in two local men, Ephraim Wilson, aged 40, of Tune Street, and Fred Wood, 34, of Dobie Street, being hospitalised due to serious burns. Unfortunately, Wood died two days later.

Walter Lodge, a coal cutter driver and his assistant, had gone to the 'B' face with the intention of repositioning the machine, arriving at about 6.20 pm. However, it appears that the trailing cable used on the previous shift had been damaged and a replacement was dispatched from the pit top. Under instructions from the overman, Horace Rawson, the new cable, some 120 yards long, was carried by ten or more men up to the face. After checks by the shift electrician (Samuel Dawson), it was attached to the machine, and his assistant (William Rushforth) was ready to put the switch in place. The air on either side of the machine had been examined for evidence of gas beforehand, with no apparent indication of any danger. Lodge shouted to Rushforth to put the power on but as soon as this took place there was a flash from the trailing cable. Still holding the switch handle, Rushforth heard numerous shouts of 'Switch off again', or similar, but the switch had tripped automatically anyway.

The flash from the trailing cable ignited firedamp, resulting in the explosion which affected Wilson and Wood. The latter appears to have been near the top waste when he was caught by the after-flame which set his clothing on fire. Nevertheless, he managed to run out by the tail gate to the level where he was overtaken by M Walsh and C Bailey by which time he was wearing a singlet, having discarded his clothes. Wrapped in a coat and given a someone else's trousers, Wood was extensively burned on both legs, both arms, his chest, back, neck and face. His mate, Wilson, also ran from the face and down the tail gate, suffering from burns to his shoulders, arms, hands and head. What a horrible experience it must have been for these two men, and indeed for their colleagues who tried to assist them.

After the explosion, overman Rawson withdrew all men from the 542 foot deep Fenton seam and also gave instructions for men to evacuate the Parkgate. On inspection of the Fenton, he found that three fires had started, a small one at the face and two others, in the waste areas or gobs. The fires were extinguished with the application of stone dust but problems and potential dangers ensued. The manager of Barrow Colliery, Mr McNeil, arrived at the B face at 9.40 pm and a junior mines inspector, Mr FH Baker, soon joined him. Also in attendance was another key figure, Mr J E Longdon, the colliery's agent and manager. McNeil returned to the surface and reported progress to his superior. But, underground, matters got worse, in terms of the air quality and heat from the gobs, causing Longden to withdraw the twenty men from the workings. A decision was then made, after consultation with George Martin, president of the local branch of the YMA, to seal off the district. It was by now midnight.

There were no prospects for the day shift men who reported for work the next morning, Tuesday. Yet some of them hung around in the pit baths rather than going home. When volunteers were required for the sandbag work underground, there was no shortage of takers, so for fairness names were 'drawn out of hat'. For some it was a very unlucky choice.

Procedures took place to build stoppings with sandbags in order top seal off the affected workings. As already mentioned, this was fairly standard procedure and had been used many times before in coal mines experiencing similar circumstances. However, the miners' representatives were critical of both the method of erection and in allowing such a large number of men (there were 62, including officials, two inspectors and rescue teams) underground in the immediate vicinity of the final sealing operations.

At 12.40 pm, some twelve hours after remedial work had begun, a major explosion of firedamp occurred. Longden, overseeing the men, and only a few yards from a stopping, later recalled, 'There was a thump and I seemed to be projected forward.' He was found unconscious, some distance away from his previous location. Eighteen men, including inspectors Houston and Baker were at or near the return stopping, the latter saying he 'Heard rumbles like three or four peels of thunder in quick succession followed by a rush of air and dust'. Fortuitously, all of these men escaped injury, though three of them were in a state of shock and taken to the surface.

Despite the best efforts of the rescue team, twelve men, all on the intake side, lost their lives. They had died in voluntary effort to make part of the pit safe for their colleagues. Particulars and circumstances of all the fatalities were listed at the end of the official report as follows:

Arthur Brown, 35, filler (asphyxia)
William Burns, 31, filler (fractured skull)
John Thomas Cocking, 38, collier (concussion and blast)
John Albert Harrott, 39, assistant manager (asphyxia and bruising)
William Hinchcliffe, 45, filler (shock and fractured ankle)
William Lakin, 55, overman (fractured skull)
Verdi Lowe, 54, filler (concussion and blast)
Robert Henry Luck, 51, overman (carbon monoxide poisioning)
George Martin, 54, repairer (carbon monoxide poisoning)
Ernest Pilkington, 37, under-manager (fractured skull and carbon monoxide poisoning)
William Rushforth, 31, filler (carbon monoxide poisoning and face injury)
Charles Wright, 41, filler (concussion and carbon monoxide poisoning)
Frederick Wood, 34, filler, (toxemia following extensive burns)

Most of the men were relatively mature miners, with an average age of forty-two.

Local press coverage of the disaster was not quite as extensive as at previous similar occasions, perhaps a consequence of wartime. Nevertheless, the *Barnsley Chronicle* reported at its first available opportunity, Saturday 21 February, using almost the whole of page 3. Advertisements on the same page included a poster from the Ritz cinema, for the film *South American George,* starring George Formby ,'singing four snappy hits'. The main disaster report praised the 'magnificent' rescue workers and included several eyewitness accounts. Thomas Bowater, aged sixteen, of 16 Gerald Road, Kendray, was one of the 'drawn out-of-the-hat' volunteers working on a stopping, and described his lucky escape:

There was a thick could of smoke all around, but recovering my senses I managed to crawl on my hands and knees towards the pit bottom. I was met by someone who helped me along. They took me to the ambulance room and I was then taken home. Had I dived the other way I should not have escaped.

Another man working on the stopping, Jack Barry (40), a filler, who lived at Pond Street, Barnsley, was knocked off his feet by the force of the blast, landing on his back, then buried, but managed to scramble to safety:

I was buried up to my neck in sand and dirt but I managed to get hold of the rail and dragged myself clear of the debris. My lamp had been buried but I rushed up the plane in the dark following some lights I could see bobbing up and down in front of me. I fell down in the plane but managed to scramble up again. I am a very lucky man to be alive.

Forty-nine-year-old Lloyd Ward, of Burton Bank, Old Mill, was described as 'another hero' in the report. A member of a neighbouring rescue team, Ward had been helping to seal off the affected district for fourteen hours when the explosion occurred. He said:

Suddenly I heard a rumble and the sealings were blown out. I was thrown along the road, but managed to crawl on my hands and knees to the pit bottom where I told some men waiting there what had happened, and they were able to rush help to the injured men. How I got myself out of the pit I don't know.

One of the volunteer stretcher bearers was said to be Charlie Hardcastle, a former feather weight boxing champion of England, who worked at the colliery.

The *Chronicle* report included short biographies and photographic portraits of several of the men who were killed, most notably Councillor George Martin, of Blenheim Avenue, Barnsley, Secretary of the Barnsley Main Branch of the YMA for the past fourteen years. Another man featured was John Albert Harrott, aged 39, underground manager at the colliery, who lived at 144 Barnsley Road, Kendray. Born at Hoyland Common, he had started work at the pit at the age of fourteen, gaining his manager's certificate in 1929.

There was due praise, too, for the speed of treatment given by the medical staff and nurses at Barnsley's Beckett Hospital, the Matron (Miss DM Lowe), saying, 'All the staff worked hard and everything went off without a hitch.' Barnsley's MP, Frank Collindridge, visited the pit and called to see the hospitalised injured.

Several of the national daily newspapers provided immediate news of the disaster. *The Times* of Wednesday, 18 February, reported that nine men had died and three were missing. A day later, the *Guardian* was able to confirm the death-toll had reached thirteen, following the death of Fred Wood in hospital, and was able to announce the establishment of the Mayor's relief fund.

The inquest on the thirteen victims was formerly opened on Thursday, 19 February, presided over by the Deputy District (Acting) Coroner, Mr SHB Gill. Representing Barrow Barnsley Main Collieries Limited, its Secretary and Director, Mr Joe Richards, expressed sympathy with the relatives of the men who had lost their lives and mentioned the speed in which the company had seven doctors on the scene. He also referred to the speed and efficiency of the first aid parties, ambulances and rescue teams and was full of praise for all the volunteer workmen 'willing to go and sacrifice their lives for their workmates'. Joe Hall, of the YMA, requested that the coroner delay any further enquiries pending any news from the Minister of Mines regarding a commission of inquiry into the cause of the disaster. After taking evidence of the identity of several victims the inquest was adjourned until 19 March, one month later.

A Disaster Fund, for providing financial aid to the dependants, was opened by the Mayor of Barnsley, Alderman Rev D Allott. Within a few days it had reached over £212 (£6,088 in today's money).

Mr & Mrs J Harrop. John Harrop was buried at Kirk Balk Cemetery, Hoyland, his funeral attended by many people.
Author's collection

MINISTRY OF FUEL AND POWER

EXPLOSIONS AT BARNSLEY MAIN COLLIERY, YORKSHIRE

REPORT

On the Causes of, and Circumstances attending the Explosions which occurred at Barnsley Main Colliery, Barnsley, Yorkshire, on the 16th and 17th February, 1942

By J. R. FELTON, O.B.E.

H.M. Deputy Chief Inspector of Mines

Presented by the Minister of Fuel and Power to Parliament by Command of His Majesty
September, 1942

LONDON
PRINTED AND PUBLISHED BY HIS MAJESTY'S STATIONERY OFFICE
To be purchased directly from H.M. STATIONERY OFFICE at the following addresses:
York House, Kingsway, London, W.C.2; 120, George Street, Edinburgh, 2;
39–41 King Street, Manchester 2; 1, St. Andrew's Crescent, Cardiff;
80, Chichester Street, Belfast;
or through any bookseller

1942

Price 1s. 3d. net

Title-page of the official inquiry into the Barnsley Main disaster of 1942. HMSO

'Barnsley Mourns Colliery Disaster Victims' was the headline in the *Barnsley Chronicle*, published on Saturday, 28 February. The report contained details of the 'black Saturday' funerals of eleven of the thirteen fatalities. Councillor Martin was the first to be buried, in Barnsley Cemetery, following a service at Holyrood Church, the largest and most high profile interment. Kendray was said to have been 'particularly hard hit by the explosion', the funerals of local men Verdi Lowe, William Rushforth and Charles Wright being held in the afternoon. Rev Rowland, Vicar of Ardsley, said that they were 'no less heroes' than war victims. A Union Jack draped the coffin of of Arthur Brown and members of the Home Guard accompanied the cortege to Barnsley Cemetery. William Burns' funeral, also at Barnsley Cemetery, had a military air, since he had been a warden of the ARP. The funeral of John Cocking was at Jump and Hemingfield Cemetery, following a service led by Canon Blakeney, the Rector of Wombwell, who said that there 'was always a danger in a miner's life'. Military honours were accorded to Ernest Pilkington, buried at Thorne, who rose from being a corporal to a deputy at Thorne Colliery, then becoming an overman at Rossington, prior to his move to Barnsley Main just seven months ago, where he was appointed under-manager. Pilkington was Captain of the Home Guard at Thorne and Barnsley. Another well-attended service and funeral took place at Hoyland, concerning Barnsley Main's underground manager, John Albert Harrott. Funerals were also reported at Worsbrough (Robert Luck) and Tankersley (William Lakin).

Funerals held on the Monday were of William Hinchcliffe and Frederick Wood, both of them being interred at Barnsley Cemetery.

The official inquiry was held, in conjunction with the adjourned inquest, at Barnsley Town Hall, on 25 March and subsequent dates, terminating (after six days of sittings) on 10 April. The inspector's report (HM Deputy Inspector JR Felton) was published and presented to the Minister of Fuel and Power; and also to Parliament, in September.

The coroner's verdict confirmed that Fred Wood died from toxaemia due to burns sustained from an ignition of gas caused by the fusing of an electric cable attached to a coal cutter. The other twelve men died from causes stated in the list of fatalities, printed above, each by 'misadventure' when working as members of a rescue party, sealing off a district in the mine which had got on fire. He concluded by saying that there had been no breach if the 1911 Coal Mines Act, either by the colliery company or the workmen. Concerning the electric trailing cable, he was of the opinion that it was not 'sufficiently examined when it arrived at the face' before the current was turned on.

The Inspector, in his observations and conclusions, confirmed that the first explosion 'was clearly one of firedamp ignited by a flash from a coal-cutter trailing cable'. He also stated that it was not possible to say that any underground inspection or test would have revealed any defect in the cable and the cable itself was unable to be recovered from the workings, making subsequent tests impossible. Expert opinion, for example from Professor Statham, of Sheffield University, was that the short-circuit was due to breakage of some of the wires of one of the cores of the cable. Regarding the presence of firedamp, the inspector was of the opinion that it *was* present along the face. He was also certain that it was an ignition of firedamp that resulted in the second major explosion. But he could not say if the presence of coal dust played any part in this and stated that sealing off dangerous areas rarely resulted in any mishap. In other words, the use of stoppings was an appropriate safety measure given the circumstances. He did recommend, however, that their correct construction should be placed in a memorandum for future usage.

(19) Barnburgh Main

Location: Barnburgh, near Mexborough
Type: Geological upheaval
Fatalities: 4
Date: Friday, 24 April 1942

When compiling both South Yorkshire mine disaster volumes, I have never ceased to be amazed at the courage and bravery of miners when endeavoring to rescue their workmates – despite great danger. The Barnburgh event, though by no means a disaster in the strictest sense of the term, was extremely unusual, in fact described as 'unique in the annals of British coal-mining' by Major HJ Humphrys, the Divisional Inspector of Mines, who had rushed to the scene. But for the rescue, it could have been far more serious. An 'earth bump', similar to an earth tremor or small earthquake, resulted in the floors lifting towards the roofs of roadways, in No 6 pit, almost half a mile underground, killing four miners and trapping thirteen others for two days. The upheaval in the north-west workings of the Parkgate seam was so great that it was recorded on seismographs as far afield as Durham, Birkenhead, Blackburn and Kew. Locally, clocks were said to have stopped, pots and pans rattled in kitchens and, more specifically, a chimney stack collapsed at a Thurnscoe house. The circumstances were recounted many years later by a local miner, Frank Vernon, in his book, *The Day the Earth Trembled* (1989).

An example of a crushed roadway but the underground scene at Barnburgh was even worse than this. Author's collection

Sometimes called jokingly the 'sunshine pit' (due to young miners apparently emptying their dudleys on their way to work on a nice day and 'laiking' ie taking an unofficial 'play day'), Barnburgh was originally sunk in 1915 as an extension to Manvers Main whose owners, Manvers Main Collieries Limited, operated the pit until nationalisation. The two Barnburgh shafts were numbered 5 and 6, the four Manvers shafts located some three miles away. No 5 was the downcast and No 6 served as the upcast. A smaller diameter third shaft (No 7) at Barnburgh, just 85 yards deep, was sunk to the Shafton seam to provide water. The main shafts accessed the Barnsley and Parkgate (or Deep) seams, at 508 and 757 yards deep respectively. Thorncliffe, Newhill, Haigh Moor and Swallow Wood coal was also accessed. At the time of the accident, Barnburgh had recently pioneered the use of skip-winding via the No 6 shaft, the Barnsley seam had just about been exhausted and there were drainage difficulties when getting the Parkgate coal. Most of the Barnburgh miners lived locally, in the Dearne valley, at Goldthorpe, Thurnscoe, Bolton-upon-Dearne, Mexborough and of course Barnburgh village itself.

A sudden movement of rock strata occurred at about 6 pm on the Friday afternoon shift, in No 6 pit, so enormous that roadways on a district in the north-west part of the workings reduced from 5 feet 6 inches in height to just 1 foot 6 inches – in less than a couple of minutes. Only one of the eighteen men working in the affected area, 42-year-old Matthew Fairhurst – managed to scramble to safety. Fairhurst was treated for shock, multiple lacerations and bruises, but was not detained at the nearest hospital (Mexborough Montagu). The risen floor crushed the coal sides of the roadways in many places, and supports, both timber and steel, were twisted and distorted. The devastation was 'almost beyond description' according to the *South Yorkshire Times and Express* of 2 May, and engineers calculated that the static weight of the strata overlying the pillared (bord and pillar working) area was calculated to be an incredible 90 million tons.

The Barnburgh Main Rescue team pictured earlier, in 1929. Norman Ellis

The Manvers, Barnburgh, and several other rescue teams and volunteers, commanded by James Bell, the colliery company's agent, made determined efforts throughout the night and following day to reach the trapped men. This involved driving through falls of rock almost equivalent to solid geology, as well as negotiating surreally distorted girders and squeezing through tight spaces, passing back excavated material by hand, via a human chain of forty men. Scratching with bare hands at times, it was truly a remarkable if not unprecedented operation, perhaps not unlike, in reverse, a great wartime escape from a Stalag camp. The pit manager, Geoffrey Payne, Major Humphrys, and assistant mines inspectors Holden and Stephenson did what they could without appreciable rest, as did Joe Hall, President of the Yorkshire Miners' Association, along with his colleagues. After 43 hours of incredible toil, eight men were reached and found to be alive and physically unhurt on the Sunday, namely J Atkins, JT Atkinson, C Chambers, E Hall, J Humphries, F Love, RH Stocks, H Wood. Nine hours later, five others were found alive: W Cruise, H Fudge, J McKenzie, LE Thompson and H Winder. Four bodies were subsequently located, one on the Monday and three on the Thursday. Their names and details were given at the inquest as:

Charles William Cope (41), collier, 72 Windhill Crescent, Mexborough
Alfred Thomas Lackenby (26), corporal, 9 Princes Road, Goldthorpe
William John Rodgers (26), collier, 73 Frederick Street, Mexborough
George Frederick Southwell (30), collier, 10 Edna Street, Bolton-upon-Dearne

John Richard Humphries, one of the first trapped men rescued, later described how, after the 'bump', he and his seven mates went back to see four full tubs squeezed between the roof, floor and sides of the roadway. The tubs presence probably saved their lives. Then there was the rescue process: first, being passed water through a small hole by the rescuers; then the hole being widened; and finally the great escape: 'We had to wriggle through on our stomachs and then crawl to a doctor who examined us and poured water on our heads and stomachs.' It had been at 8 pm on the Saturday when they first heard tapping sounds and shouted back. More tapping was heard on the Sunday about midday and they were eventually released at 1.10 pm the same day. A young haulage lad, William (or Wilfred) Cruise (19), described how he and his even younger mate, Leslie Thompson, managed to get down the crossgate and release from a fall of rock the deputy, Walter Winder. They then met Fudge and saw Lackerby who was dead. They had no water by Saturday, so Cruise retrieved some from dudleys abandoned earlier. This involved getting through tight spaces. Cruise and Thompson were congratulated by the coroner for their bravery. Winder, limping into the witness box, explained how Cruise got him out from a pile of debris, almost buried alive. Joe Hall, referred to Cruise as 'a modest young man' whose action was 'one of the most courageous feats he had come across in his varied experience of pit disasters'.

Geoffrey Payne, the manager of Barnburgh Main, gave evidence at the inquest for over two hours. He explained how, in the previous few months, there had been problems with the floor lifting in the Parkgate seam but thought that the disaster was the result of a 'shock bump'. But concern was expressed by several rescue team members regarding the movement of strata in the many months before the disaster.

A verdict of 'accidental death' was given for all four of the victims of the Barnburgh disaster, Major Humphrys paying particular tribute to the rescue workers, whose 'indomitable spirit of endurance and perseverance' made him 'proud to be associated with the mining industry'.

In an interview with the *South Yorkshire Times*, the YMA President, Joe Hall, spoke about all the miners involved, saying, 'Never have I been prouder of the men I represent.' Hall also paid tribute to Major Humphrys, referring to him as 'a man of rare courage who was daunted by neither personal danger nor difficulty', an exceptional compliment from a union man to an inspector. Despite Hall's pleas, there was no separate official inquiry. However, a report published by Humphrys, in December 1942, confirmed the view that the upheaval was a result of a 'shock bump', even though such an occurrence in the UK had never been previously recorded. Amongst the possible contributory factors mentioned was the great depth and method of working, the strength of the coal seam and the floor, the size of the pillars and the extent of extracted areas.

More examples of eyewitness reports are given in Frank Vernon's book, referred to above, and of course there are still local people who either remember some aspects of the event or have family connections with the victims, rescued and rescuers. Edmund 'Ted' Lunness was a fifteen-year-old pit lad at Barnburgh in 1942. In 2004 he spoke to me about his memories of the disaster, when he was learning First Aid in his spare time:

> … we were having practice at the Reform Club, Goldthorpe. Senior members of the brigade were there, along with some members of the [Barnburgh] rescue team … An urgent message came through. There had been an accident at the pit and ambulance men and rescuers were needed straight away. We juniors tagged along and when we got to the pit I was given the job to take food and water to the base for the rescuers: corned beef sandwiches in a biscuit tin and ten-pint dudleys of water. It was classified as a 'big bump', where the strata broke – the Parkgate rock – coming down with such a force that caused the floor to come up in the roadways … There were a lot of very brave men, a lot were rescued. The men that came out were in a bad state as they had been working in very hot and dusty areas.

Anyone reading this section of the book cannot help but appreciate the tremendous bravery of the rescue workers and the tenacity of the trapped men. Despite subsequent changes in working methods at Barnburgh, the lasting legacy of the Barnburgh disaster is the great heroism of all those directly involved which is why this event has been included here.

Edward 'Ted' Lunness, aged sixteen, with the McLaughlinn Cup, awarded in a First Aid competition and presented at Worsbrough Bridge, 1943. E Lunness

Courrieres

The most remarkable story of survival after entombment occurred following the Courrieres disaster, near Lens, in northern France, on 10 March 1906, when 1,099 men and boys were killed. This remains Europe's worst mine disaster. Thirteen men were found gaunt, but still alive, twenty days after the explosion. They had survived by eating the food they had taken underground, slaughtering and eating pit ponies, even consuming bark from timber props. Incredibly, a final survivor was found four days later. The two eldest men were awarded the *Legion d'honneur* and the others the *Medaille d'or de courage*.

(20) Manvers Main

Location: Wath-upon-Dearne, Rotherham
Type: Explosion
Fatalities: 5
Date: Sunday, 4 March 1945

Three years after the Barnburgh incident, the Manvers Main Colliery Company suffered another wartime multiple fatality, this time at its flagship colliery which, after nationalisation, became one of the largest coal and coke complexes in Europe. An explosion in the Meltonfield seam resulted in the deaths of five men, named as:

Bertram John Conroy   John Kelsey
Raymond Kelsey   Charles Edward Leeman
John Ollett

Manvers Main, photographed by Scrivens of Doncaster. Chris & Pearl Sharp/Old Barnsley

The Meltonfield coal was, on average, 3ft 4in thick and, at 122 yards deep, the shallowest seam exploited at Manvers, worked by electronically operated coal-cutters and belt conveyors. Of the four shafts, the No 1 (downcast) and No 4 (upcast) served the Meltonfield and Haigh Moor seams respectively, the latter at 347 yards depth. Geoffrey Payne was now agent for both Barnburgh and Manvers; and Mr EJ Kimmins managed Manvers, assisted by two under-managers, Mr A Wild being responsible for the No 1 pit where the accident happened. The district in which the explosion occurred had been visited by Kimmins on 1 February and by Wild on on 17 February, about one to three weeks before the accident.

The Meltonfield coal, in the North-Eastern part of the colliery, was not considered a gassy seam though ignitions had occurred during working at other sites. However, in the North district as a whole firedamp was recorded on thirteen occasions in the six months before the explosion, but mostly when the auxiliary fan had disfunctioned or when the tubing was damaged by roof falls. At Manvers there had been problems working this seam intensively due to water coming through the roof from rocks above, so power loading and a pillar and wall system were abandoned in favour of a retreated (US-style) longwall operation. The district was being opened up by driving twin 13ft-wide parallel roads with connections (or 'slits') at intervals of 36 yards.

Since there were no survivors of the men at work on the affected area it was not possible to ascertain the exact circumstances of the explosion. However, details concerning earlier shifts, and in particular the previous afternoon shift, helped to place matters in context. During the weekend modifications were underway in the method of conveying coal in the 6s and 7s headings, overseen by the day overman, Harold Mann. This involved the movement and installation conveyors and associated equipment. On the Saturday, the day shift deputy, Frank Dobson, had made inspections in the North-West district and found the air in order, with no evidence of firedamp in the headings. The Saturday afternoon shift deputy, Laurence Wroe, had 43 men working in the North district, 18 of whom were in the North-West and also found that the air was in good order, though he did not feel it was necessary to check the headings. The auxiliary fan was not running, having been stopped by a shot-firer, assistant deputy, Fred Crossley. A problem occurred regarding a Joy loader, the operator, John Wilson, saying that 'the cable got trapped in between [the machine] and the gearhead of the chain conveyor'. The slack cable in front of the loader got fast and there was a flash and the electric current cut. It was 4.30 pm. Inspection of the cable showed it had been punctured but Crossley did not notice this extended through the rubber into one of the cores.

Before the above incident Crossley had found that the fan had stopped,suggesting to him that the current had tripped. In the absence of an electrician on duty he restored the power, reporting the problem which had occurred to deputy Wroe and saying that an electrician was needed. The onsetter was told that an electrician would be informed the next morning. Crucially, the Joy loader connecting cable had not been completely disconnected even though a report sheet said that it had.

Harry Ayscough, the deputy on duty during the night shift of Saturday 3 March, had descended the pit at midnight (instead of the usual time of 10 pm) with nine workmen: four to cut 8B north face, four to move conveyor pans and one (Charles Leeman) to attend to the three pumps. Electric power was switched on for the 8B face but the men only had electric lamps, with no safety lamps or detectors with them, nor had the other four men any gas testing equipment. Leeman did have a safety lamp but this was found at the pumphouse after the explosion. Ayscough tested for gas by the fan, found none, so it was

Veteran Manvers Main miner Sidney Cutts, who was interviewed in 2003. The author

switched on after seven hours of inactivity. The four men dispatched to move pans in the North Plane (Conroy, the two Kelseys and Ollett) and Leeman were not seen alive again. Making his second inspection, beginning at 2.35 am, Ayscough noticed something was amiss when he saw that the main belt was covered in dust and haze and dust was showing in his lamp. Moving towards the area where the face men were located, there had been a fall of rock on to the conveyor and he found difficulty in breathing, therefore had to retreat. Stumbling and crawling for help, he lost consciousness for some time and managed to get to 8B face where men were still at work, one of them, Ben Winder, was instructed to telephone management that something serious had happened and to send in a rescue team. The first rescue team descended the pit at 6.25 am and an upturned tub provided further clear evidence of an explosion. Work proceeded in relays to establish a fresh air base, repair stoppings and make roadways safe for travel, the men wearing breathing apparatus. Rescue men and mines inspectors found progression halted by heavy falls of roof.

It was only by 8 March that access to headings, without using breathing apparatus, was possible and a great deal of devastation was found. The last body, that of Charles Leeman, was found lying under a conveyor belt, a week later, on 16 March.

Veteran Manvers miner Sidney Cutts (b.1919) recalled the 1942 disaster (and accidents in general) when he spoke to me in an interview, recorded in 2003:

> I was at home … They wanted volunteers, so me and Joe [Toft] went to the pit. There was nothing we could do … but when we got halfway along the district we got news that three [dead miners] were being brought up … we were told not to look … I knew them all. We started to look for Charlie Leeman but it was a couple of weeks before he was found. A man shovelling on a belt found him underneath. I witnessed many accidents when I was a deputy … there were some really bad ones. One young chap was killed on the face … he'd been sat down and you had not noticed the roof coming down; and was buried with his head on his knees. You almost got hardened to it.

The inquest on the deaths of the Manvers victims was held in conjuction with the official inquiry, 23–30 May, at Wath-upon-Dearne Town Hall. The coroner was Alan C Lockwood and the inquiry was conducted by Mr JR Felton, OBE. Twenty-two witnesses were heard. Northumberland-born Sir John Robinson Felton was the HM Chief Inspector of Mines (in the Ministry of Fuel and Power) and had reported on the Barnsley Main explosions, five years earlier, in 1942. In his early career he was an apprentice mining engineer and then certified manager at West Stanley Colliery in Durham and Stobswood Colliery, Northumberland.

In each of the five cases, the coroner found a verdict of 'misadventure', details as follows: Raymond Kelsey, asphyxia due to carbon monoxide poisoning and 'shock of burns'; John Ollett and John Kelsey the same; Bertram Conroy, a depressed fracture of the skull; and Charles Leeman, shock of burns, multiple crushing, fractures to the cranium, thorax and chest. The coroner stated that all men were involved in an explosion of firedamp in the Meltonfield seam but there was not sufficient evidence 'to determine conclusively' all the circumstances. However, it was confirmed that the explosion was of firedamp and coal dust played little or no part; also that it originated in 7s heading near the Joy loader; furthermore, the igniting medium was an electronic flash or spark from a short circuit in the trailing cable feeding the loader. The inquiry drew attention to the use of auxiliary fans and recommended that managers should draw up a simple code of rules for the instruction of officials and workmen dealing with such matters.

Part Eight

The Last Disasters
1947–78

"This tragedy may remind people, as it has reminded me, that there is still a very high price to be paid in human life for the coal we get in this country."

Tony Benn MP, Secretary of State for Energy,
speaking after the Houghton Main disaster, in 1975

After the nationalisation of the coal industry, vesting day being 1 January 1947, the number of accidents in our coal mines generally declined, deaths being halved within ten years. Safety in mines was given far more prominence, with uniform procedures for all National Coal Board collieries. Emphasis began to turn towards longer term industrial disease,

Arthur Scargill (left) and Tony Benn at Houghton Main in 1975. Barnsley Chronicle

particularly respiratory ailments; this in the context of increasing usage of electronic coal-cutting machines with their high dust discharges. But there continued to be a desperate shortage of coal, especially during the exceptionally bad winter of 1947. Coal was central to Britain's post-war industrial recovery. A Five Day Week was introduced as an incentive, the men paid as though they had worked six days as a bonus on the completion of all shifts.

The start of a new beginning for the industry also marked the reorganisation of the mining unions, amalgamating into the National Union of Mineworkers just after the war. *A Plan for Coal* was drawn up in 1950, leading to the rationalisation of the coal industry and expenditure on modernising pits achieved record levels.

Post-war legislation was slow. The landmark, but thirty-six-year-old Coal Mines Act (1911) was not repealed and replaced until many aspects of the industry were covered by the comprehensive Mines and Quarries Act of 1954. A further statute, the Mines and Quarries (Tips) Act of 1969, was a reaction to the terrible Aberfan disaster of 1966, when 116 children and 28 adults were killed at a South Wales village primary school, overwhelmed by an unstable pit heap.

However, big mine disasters were not confined to the past in some coalfield areas. On 15 August, only a few months after nationalisation, a disaster at the William pit, near Whitehaven in Cumbria, resulted in 104 fatalities.

Locally, the explosion at Barnsley Main, only six months an NCB colliery, killed seven men and injured more than twenty others. The resultant editorial in the *Barnsley Chronicle* captured the grim mood of the time, but concluded with some optimism:

> There are moments in the affairs of men which defy any human powers of expression to interpret feelings aroused by such tragic events … The disaster … has shocked the entire nation and underlined … the odds against which the miner works … these men did not die in vain, if the nature of their end stimulates new research efforts into ways and means of reducing mining fatalities, even below the comparatively low figure at which they stand today.

On 11 November of the same year, three men lost their lives in the Winter seam, in a roof fall at Wombwell. For his bravery during this accident, rescue team member Walter Holroyd Lee was awarded the Edward Medal (Bronze, later converted to the George Medal). Walt brought two casualties to the surface and then went underground for a second time, carrying out two of the dead, a remarkable act of bravery. Then, on 19 September 1950, a rock fall killed another three men at Grimethorpe. Not too far away from South Yorkshire, on 26 September 1950, 80 men died in a major underground fire at Cresswell, in Derbyshire; and on 29 May the following year, 83 fatalities (including two rescue men) were recorded at Easington, in Durham, one of the most modern collieries in Britain.

By the mid to late 1950s miners and management had achieved such a surplus of production that coal was stocked in great piles in many coalfield areas due to falling demand, in the wake of relatively cheap oil. Clean Air Acts contributed to this process. The chairmanship of Lord Robins (1961–71) at the NCB resulted in a strategic contraction of the British coal industry, with 400 pits closed; its demise accelerated to near oblivion after the 1984/85 miners' strike and during the pit closures and return to privatisation in the 1990s.

As far as post-war South Yorkshire was concerned there were no colliery disasters, at least officially, after the Second World War, and certainly no major ones. As already mentioned, for an accident to be classed as a disaster there had to be more than ten fatalities.

The Silverwood pit paddy accident almost reached this category but, as before, I have felt it appropriate for this and several other post-war multiple fatality accidents to be included in this final section. The very late ones, in particular, were given widespread media coverage and, of course, remain in the memories of many people, including several of my relatives. Indeed, objective interpretation of all surviving and accessible evidence may be best evaluated by future historians. What follows is simply a case by case overview of the last multiple fatality accidents to impact on the affected families and communities of South Yorkshire.

(21) Barnsley Main

Location: Barnsley
Type: Explosion
Fatalities: 9
Date: Wednesday, 7 May 1947

The accident happened at 12. 15 pm, towards the end of the day, or 'filling' shift, in the No 3 district of the pit, in a newly developed seam: the Kent Thick. It occurred on the third working day, following the introduction of the Five Day Week and only five years after the 1942 disaster. All the injured were conveyed to Barnsley Beckett Hospital.

Immediate news appeared in the national press the following day, Thursday 8 May, *The Times'* report, for instance, was under the headline BARNSLEY COLLIERY EXPLOSION. It included reference to a joint statement from Major General Sir Noel Holmes, Chairman of the North East Divisional Coal Board and Joe Hall, President of the Yorkshire Mineworkers' Federation, in which sympathy was expressed to the relatives and management of the colliery.

More extensive coverage understandably appeared in the *Barnsley Chronicle* whose main headline (on page 8) related to the circumstances of the ignition, as: PIT SWEPT BY SHEET OF FLAME AFTER EXPLOSION. The pit top scene and rescue was described in all too familiar detail:

> Soon after news of the disaster had spread, wives and other relatives were keeping vigil and there were poignant scenes as, after the injured had been rushed to hospital in a fleet of ambulances, stretchers bearing the dead were carried from the pit-head to the first aid room which served as a temporary mortuary.
>
> So expeditiously did the gallant band of men toil underground that by 4 pm the last body had been brought to the surface. All the men known to be down had then been accounted for and the rescue teams were able to withdraw.

Survivors interviewed spoke about 'a violent rush of air', so powerful that it 'hurled men six or eight yards', and was followed by 'a pall of dust-laden choking fumes'. But one unnamed rescue worker was quoted as saying, 'Down there you could not tell there has been an explosion at all. I saw no sign of any fall of roof and there was not a ton of dirt at the coal face where the explosion occurred.'

Five rescue teams were involved, namely Barnsley Main, Monk Bretton (two teams), Woolley and Wharncliffe Woodmoor, all under the direction of JE Parkinson, superintendent of the Barnsley Mines Rescue Station. The latter was located in the town, off Eastgate, at Falcon Street. The assistant superintendent there, Rowland Noble, was one of the brave rescue workers who took part in what must have been a dangerous and distressing operation. The condition of the dead miners was described as 'terribly burned' by one of the rescue men.

Among key people who went down to inspect the affected workings were WH Dixon (the pit's manager), J Atkinson (under-manager), Councillor TS Brown (NUM delegate,

---

Nine dead, 21 injured — Barnsley Main survivors say—

PIT SWEPT BY SHEET OF FLAME AFTER EXPLOSION

They waited....

A **GENERAL** view of the pithead as crowds gathered to await news of those involved in the disaster.

Nine men were killed and 21 injured by a silent flash and a sheet of flame which swept underground workings 720 feet below ground at Barnsley Main Colliery on Wednesday.

The explosion in No. 3 district of the Kent thick seam—a seam which was only opened up about 12 months ago—occurred about 12.15 p.m., shortly before the day workers were due to finish the shift. The disaster on the third working day following the introduction of the Five Day Week was reminiscent of a similar calamity at Barnsley Main in 1942 and cast a gloom over the whole town and district.

Soon after news of the disaster had spread wives and other relatives were keeping vigil and there were poignant scenes as, after the injured had been rushed to hospital in a fleet of ambulances, stretchers bearing the dead were carried from the pithead to the first aid room which served as a temporary mortuary.

So expeditiously did the gallant band of men toil underground that by 4 p.m. the last body had been brought to the surface. All the men known to be down had then been accounted for and the rescue teams were able to be withdrawn.

The accident is believed to have been caused by the sparking of an electric underground cable, one theory being that there was a flash which ignited coal-dust, most of the men suffering burns from the sheet of flame, although there was no actual fire.

Survivors all speak of a violent rush of air hurling men six or eight yards and a pall of dust-laden choking fumes.

One rescue worker returning to the surface described the explosion as a mystery. "Down there," he said, "you could not tell there has been any explosion at all. I saw no sign of any fall of roof and there was not a ton of dirt at the coal face where the explosion occurred.

The air is now fresh. The first rescue party wore oxygen breathing apparatus but we have just managed without any apparatus at all. It is four minutes walk from the bottom of the pit shaft to the scene of the explosion. No fire followed the flash but most of the victims are suffering from burns."

Nine Dead

The list of dead is:—
Harry Storey (31), colliery deputy, married, 117, Colley-crescent, Kendray.
Arthur Edwards (54), miner, married, 47, Rock-street, Barnsley.
Joseph Blaydon (26), miner, single, 63, Neville-avenue, Park House Estate.
William Peake (47), miner, married, 30, Creswell-street, Pogmoor.
Clifford Allen (34), miner, married, 9, Chapel-street, Ardsley.
Harry Crowcroft (26), miner, single, 10, Grange-lane, Cundy Cross.
Harry Irwin Baxter (25), miner, married, 8, Castle-street, Barnsley.
Ernest Earnshaw (53), miner, married, 63, Summer-lane, Barnsley.
John Denton (45), miner, married, 29, Queen's-road, Barnsley.

The injured

Injured and detained in hospital are:—
Leslie Greaves (27), 32, Birk-road, Kendray.
Alec Spence (26), 48, Thornton-road, Kendray.
Ernest Markwell (19), 21, Industry-road, Stairfoot.
Gordon Grocott (15), 34, Doncaster-road, Barnsley.
Everall Lawton (16), 21 Albion-terrace, Barnsley.
Charles Rigby (17), 78, Upper Sheffield-road, Barnsley.
John Chambers (35), 36, Birk-road, Kendray.
Frank Ridge (20), 39, Albion-road, Stairfoot.
Peter Scuffham (16), Obelisk House, Church-st., Barnsley.
Stanley Lea (27), 50, Lambert-road, Kendray.
William Haigh (44), 93, Darley-avenue, Ward Green.
Frank Burton (15), 61, Don-

In the shadow of one of Barnsley's best-known landmarks, the Barnsley Main spoil heap (Barnsley's "mountain"), there were harrowing scenes as anxious parents, relatives and sweethearts anxiously waited for news of the loved ones.

Their stoic attitude could not hide the chill in their hearts; neither could the brilliance of May sun thaw it.

Each time the headgear wheels turned hopes and fears struggled for supremacy; there was a murmur as the cage ascended followed by distressing silence, a stretcher party slowly passing towards the silent watchers.

Relatives were seeking clues to identity any uncovered clothes and one clearly heard a whispered prayer of thankfulness the tragic parties passed at irregular intervals. So far all had worn boots—a pair of clogs were being sought.

Finally there was no prayer, silence was unbroken, and one saw the tragic blasting of hopes as the gaze travelled along the blanket covering the shod feet. These were the clogs....

Mr. and Mrs Walter Allsop, Priory-road, Lundwood, with Frank, waited almost three hours. Their son, Raymond (18), was known to be working on that face. As bodies were recovered they were told there was little hope for any remaining below ground.

A workman recognised the clogs and one had to see their faces to imagine the intense relief they felt when he told them Raymond had come out of the pit, and was not thought to be seriously hurt.

They had seen seven bodies carried by, and tears welled in the eyes of motherly Mrs. Allsop; great was her relief.

She had not heard any other news of Raymond until called to his bedside—he is one of the seriously ill.

Another tragic figure on the pithead was the father of Harry Crowcroft. Though encased in plaster cast as a result of accident in which he sustained injuries to his spine, he waited to hear of his son.

It was a distraught parent who had to be led away when he was told his son had been killed.

Local coverage of the 1947 Barnsley Main disaster in the town's newspaper. Barnsley Chronicle

Mines' rescue team outside their Barnsley headquarters, Falcon Street. Jack Faulkner

Barnsley Main), Professor KN Atkinson and J Longden (general managers), R McNeil (area deputy general manager), E Hoyle (agent), Major Humphrys and Major HS Hudspeth (Divisional Inspectors of Mines), John Hunter (NCB production director); and, of course, the miners' trade union leader Joe Hall (now a veteran of 36 disasters and president of the Yorkshire Area NUM), brave as ever, whose comments afterwards included the following:

> When I got down shortly after 1.30 I found the dust which had hampered rescue in the first place clearing. I was able to lead the rescue teams straight to the centre of the explosion area. The dead men were badly burned and had been killed by blast and asphyxiation. Most of them must have died instantly.

Joe also spoke about finding his 'old friend' Harry Storey 'with whom I had worked on previous rescue jobs … knocked out near the coal face'. Despite attempt at first aid, Storey was dead before they could get him to the surface. Storey, a shot-firer and deputy, was an experienced member of the Barnsley Main rescue team, the last body to be recovered. Still feeling unwell from a previous accident, his wife had begged him not to go to work on the fateful shift. Clifford Allen, another of the unlucky victims, had 'rushed to work' according to his widow, so as to ensure that he worked his five days to qualify for six days' pay.

Despite the deaths, the colliery resumed work (apart from the affected face) the very next day, Thursday.

The inquest was held before the Deputy West Riding District Coroner, Mr SHB Gill and occupied four full days of evidence and submissions from 24 individuals. Some of the graphic stories came from those injured by the blast, including several young miners. John Peter Scuffham, surveyor's assistant, aged fifteen, explained to the coroner that he was taking sights with his instrument when there was a flash which filled the whole of the gate (roadway) front, saying 'I felt myself going backwards and when I came to I was on my back. I could hear voices and and then I fell over someone crawling on his hands and knees.' Scuffham also told how he came across sixteen-year-old Kenneth Haigh who was groaning and unable to walk, and then, with the help of another fifteen-year-old, Gordon Grocock,

The grim task of volunteers: carrying the bodies of workmates after the disaster.
Barnsley Chronicle

Tired rescue men return to the surface. Barnsley Chronicle

helped Haigh to safety. Another boy miner, Frank Barron, aged sixteen, described how he was working on the pan switch when he was thrown about ten yards down the gate. Joe Hall, in his usual style, questioned the colliery electrician concerning the fusing of an electric cable (said to be the cause of the explosion by expert witnesses).

The coroner's verdict, issued on the Thursday, included the following:

> The jury think the electric cable ought to be examined at least once every shift by a competent electrician and they don't feel quite satisfied that it has been handled as it should have been.

A 'death by misadventure' verdict was recorded for all nine of the deceased miners but there was also a very serious comment of 'gross negligence' in respect of running a machine 'without the cover' which was designed to prevent an accident...' Joe Hall even hinted at industrial action, saying, 'If the men in the pits around here stop working tomorrow you will realise the seriousness of it'. However, the coroner was of the opinion that there was no case for 'criminal' neglect.

The official inquiry was published on 11 December 1947, the work of the experienced Divisional Inspector of Mines, Major HJ Humphrys, and presented to the Minister of Fuel and Power, Hugh Gaitskell MP. The source of the ignition was said to be due to an arc formed between the cores of the trailing cable and a moving nut on the rocker arm of the driving gear of the shaker conveyor. The rocker's protective cover was missing, it's presence would have prevented damage to the cable which was the direct cause of the explosion. The opening of a ventilation door by a surveying team caused gas to be moved towards the trailing cable. The report's recommendations included the appointment of a ventilation engineer.

It was ironic that both Barnsley Main explosions related to cables.

Details of the fatalities were given as:

Clifford Allen (34), collier, married, 9 Chapel Street, Ardsley
Harry Irwen Baxter (25), collier, married, 8 Castle Street, Barnsley
Joseph Blaydon (26), collier, single, 63 Neville Avenue, Park House Estate
Harry Crowcroft (26), collier, single, 10 Grange Lane, Cundy Cross
John Denton (45), collier, married, 29 Queen's Road, Barnsley
Ernest Earnshaw (53), collier, married, 63 Summer Lane, Barnsley
Arthur Edwards (54), collier, married, 47 Rock Street, Barnsley
William Peake (47), repairer, married, 30 Cresswell Street, Pogmoor
Harry Storey (31), deputy, married, 117 Colley Crescent, Kendray

Two men, Syd Blackburn (shot-firer) and Harry Crummack (chargeman filler), were presented with the George Cross for their bravery during the Barnsley Main disaster, at Buckingham Palace, in December 1947. They led a group of men to safety before returning to save the lives of James Barrow and John Hirst; and were said to have been prepared to carry on helping, until relieved by the arrival of the mines rescue team.

(22) Barnburgh Main

Location: Barnburgh, near Mexborough
Type: Explosion
Fatalities: 6
Date: Friday, 26 June 1957

More than ten years were to elapse before a substantial accident took place in South Yorkshire mines, when an explosion and its aftermath resulted in the deaths of six men at Barnburgh Main colliery, the scene of the infamous 'earth bump' and 'entombment' of 1942.

Barnburgh was now in the No 2 Area of the North Eastern Division of the NCB, employing about 2,000 men underground and producing 4,500 tons of coal a day. Mr H Heap (Area General, appointed 1 June 1957), Mr CAS Moore (Area Production), Mr F Darley (Deputy Area Production, Operations), Mr WT Marsh (Deputy Area Production, planning), Mr J Ford (Group), Mr S Beaumont (Manager), Mr R Edwards (Under-manager, Parkgate) and Mr W Hayselden (Under-manager, Newhill) were the principal officials associated with the colliery.

The explosion occurred in the North West No 1 District (one of seven producing districts) of the Newhill seam, which had been worked for ten years and was 4ft thick. The coal was extracted here (by longwall advancing faces), via cutting machines and blasting, hand-filled onto a face conveyor, and transported underground to skip bunkers which were hauled up the shaft. The affected face normally yielded 430 tons per shift and was ventilated by a separate split from the main intake. The firemen's records indicated that firedamp had not been reported in the district during the previous three months; however, an inspection on 19 June, a week before the explosion, revealed an explosive mixture of gas in a cavity in the roof on the left side of the main intake.

On the afternoon of 26 June, the afternoon shift deputy, Robert Ashton, took over from his colleague, J Triffit, who found everything (apart from a faulty telephone) in good order. All work proceeded normally, getting ready for the wastemen to start on the afternoon shift, at 2.30 pm. Men on the split shift consisted of six back rippers, three conveyor turners, one steel checker and two gate belt extenders; also present were two surveyor's assistants, Charlesworth and Silcock, who were near the face, extending the roadway lines. Charlesworth was the only man in the district with a flame safety lamp.

Under Ashton's authority and supervision, two men were preparing to fire a shot and had protected a power cable with a piece of old belting, laid beneath the roof that was to be blasted. The usual precautions were taken and the shot was fired. Almost immediately this was followed by a 'hissing sound' and 'spurt of flame'. A large fall of stone had crashed onto the power cable which caused it to be damaged, a flash apparently coming from the resultant live point. The flame travelled inbye and was followed by a blast which raised great clouds of dust. The back rippers were told to crawl along the conveyor belt to safety, due to the poor visibility. Ashton subsequently came across several walking wounded men.

Outside the affected area, an afternoon deputy, R Nelson, experienced a sudden blast of air as he travelled to the North district and telephoned the overman, F Allsop, who was in the box hole office, near the pit bottom. Approaching the affected face, Nelson found conditions too thick with dust to progress with safety. Allsop issued orders for all miners to withdraw from the seam and, with the assistance of an electrician, Colin Rodgers, all the switches were turned off. Eventually, they reached the area where the shot had been fired, finding more injured men at the face, though visibility was down to two or three yards. Morphia was given to the badly injured miners. As many as twenty men who had been at work on the main conveyor suffered from burns, the last taken to the surface at 4.50 pm, two hours after the explosion. Nineteen of the injured were detained in hospital and six of these subsequently died, named as:

Richard Corbridge (35), belt turner
Herbert Fells (41), wasteman
Joseph Hill (55), back ripper
David Lunness (48), wasteman (uncle of Ted Lunness, quoted in the 1942 Barnburgh
    disaster section; and at the Cortonwood entry, below)
Charles Trevor Scott (32), belt turner
Derek Smith (28), wasteman

The coroner's inquest on the deaths of five of the men who resided in his Rotherham jurisdiction, opened on 17 September and returned a 'misadventure' verdict. The jury recommended to the Minister of Power that regulations should be altered in order to make it compulsory for rigid protection to be afforded to any power cable liable to be damaged following a shot.

A second inquest took place, on 24 September, on the sixth victim, a 'misadventure' verdict again being returned. The jury also recommended 'definite instructions and regulations' be laid down in respect of the protection of live cables prior to shot-firing.

The official inquiry was led by the the Divisional Inspector of Mines, Mr CW Scott, CBE, who presented his report to the Minister of Power, Lord Mills, in October 1957. The inquiry found that the firing of the shot had not ignited the gas. The electric cable was found to be damaged, and also the cable feeding from the transformer to the switch gear near the face was faulty; but the fault was located where the cable had been buried by debris. This resulted in a short circuit which had blown a hole in the outer casing of the armoured cable which was the source of the explosion. The cable should have been properly protected, according to existing regulations.

(23) Cortonwood

Location: Brampton, near Wombwell
Type: Emmision of gas
Fatalities: 4
Date: Monday, 19 June 1961

Five men were killed in an explosion at Walton, near Wakefield, on 22 April 1959 but the next serious accident to take place in the modern county of South Yorkshire was at Cortonwood Colliery in 1961. First developed in the 1870s, Cortonwood was not far from one of the most tragic pit disasters in British coalmining history, at Lundhill Colliery (see volume 1), when 189 men and boys were killed. Cortonwood later became famous – at least in journalistic terms – as 'the pit that sparked the 1984/85 miners' strike'.

Cortonwood had undergone a great deal of modernization by the late 1950s and, at the time of the accident, in 1961, a new coal preparation plant was being developed, as well as

BARNSLEY CHRON
& South Yorkshire News

and incorporating the "Barnsley Independent"

ESTABLISHED 1858

Telephone 3667 (five lines)

VOL. CII, 5815

REGISTERED AT THE GENERAL POST
OFFICE FOR TRANSMISSION BEYOND
THE UNITED KINGDOM

A.B.C. CERTIFIED NET SALES, DEC. 31, 1960, 40,588 COPIES WEEKLY

FIVE EDITIONS COVERING TOWN, WOMBWELL, HOYLAND, PENISTONE, CUDWORTH, ROYSTON AND GRIM

FOUR DIE IN COLLIERY TRAGEDY

BUT EIGHT ARE SAVED AS RESCUERS TOIL ALL NIGHT

DEATH came to Cortonwood Colliery on Monday, when a pocket of methane gas burst deep down in the 9's South face of the Silkstone seam, catching 12 miners unawares. While rescuers toiled for 11 hours through the night, four men died and eight were brought out alive. These included the overman and the deputy, who risked death trying to reach their colleagues and drag them out of the killer gas.

The dead men are: Robert Arnott, aged 33, of 35, Welland-crescent, Elsecar; John Kellett, aged 38, 43, Rufford-avenue, Athersley, Barnsley; Albert Bailey, aged 48, 7, Dearne-road, Brampton, and John Holmes, aged 46, 15, Cliffe-road, Brampton.

Bailey and Holmes, both of them machine team men, had worked all their lives at Cortonwood Colliery.

The men who escaped with their lives are: Alfred Catlin, aged 47, married with three children, of 15, Chapel-avenue, Brampton; Morgan Clayton, aged 24, married, 63, Broomhead-road, Wombwell; Granville Mason, aged 54, married 7, Cliffewood, Brampton.

"He turned towards the gate and saw that it was, as he called it, 'Dancing.' There were violent vibrations of the roof. He shouted to the men to come out.

"Three men had come off the face, when Mr. Gibbons realised that the ventilation had become stationary, and then started to reverse.

"His oil lamp went out, and he tripped out all the electric switches.

"There has been a very heavy weight with a large omission of gas, which is now slowly clearing." (This statement was made at 2.45 a.m. on Tuesday).

The four dead men were overcome on the face, and were the last to be reached by the

The sombre front-page headline about the Cortonwood accident. Barnsley Chronicle

Granville Mason, with blackened face, was one of the men trapped following the gas emission and roof fall. His wife, Annie (also seen here), anxiously waiting at the surface. Barnsley Chronicle

Eric Crabtree, who helped with the rescue operations at Cortonwood. The author

Rescue team return to the surface at Cortonwood. Eric Crabtree is second right. Eric Crabtree

electrification and progression to skip-winding. Silkstone and Haigh Moor coal was wound from No 1 (downcast) shaft, 14–15,000 tons produced from a workforce of 1,500 men.

It was very warm and sunny in Brampton on 24 June 1961, though for many miners working on the afternoon shift the day became a nightmare, resulting in tragedy. The accident happened when a pocket of methane gas burst in the 9s South face of the Silkstone seam, catching twelve miners unawares. Rescue workers toiled all night and managed to bring out eight men alive. Cadeby miner and mines rescue man Eric Crabtree (b.1932, also see Part Two, relating to the Cadeby disaster, above) recalled the all-night rescue operations when he spoke to me in 2004:

> I had been on afternoons that day. There had been a big inrush of gas … We were about to go to bed when I got the call. We went underground about 12.30 am, wearing breathing apparatus. There was a lot of gas, even in an airlock at No 2 shaft on the surface. None of the bodies had come out. The Cortonwood team had done a survey first. We retrieved one body, a big chap called Bob Arnott, found dead on a panza chain. The seam was only 2ft 6 inch high, so it took two hours to get him off … more dead were further away but we had used most of our Proto oxygen. We stayed at the fresh air base on standby until another team took us off. It was 8 am when we came out.

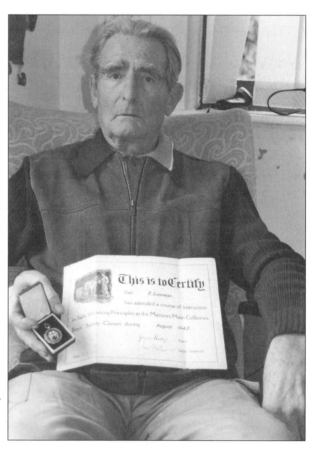

Ted Lunness, the former manager of Cortonwood Colliery, recalls the disaster.
The author

Cotonwood had a new young manager, thirty-four-year-old Ted Lunness, who spoke to me in 2004 with controlled emotion when he recalled the day, evening, long night and morning of the accident at 'his' pit:

I went to work for eight in the morning and came home about five, had my meal, when the phone rang. It was the under-manager of the Silkstone [seam], old Jack Hunter, a wonderful man. He informed me that there had been an emission of gas and all the roadways were full of methane. The rescue teams were sent for but, unfortunately for me, my boss, the Group Manager, the Area Deputy Production Manager and Production Manager had all gone to a meeting and were not available. I rang Joe Ford, the neighbouring Group Manager … He and Fred Steel, the Manager at Manvers, came over to assist me. I informed the inspectorate, the police, and the press soon got to know. We got the ambulance and rescue men organised as soon as possible. Jack Hunter managed to communicate with some men in the return gate, telling them to turn the compressed air on and to huddle on the floor. This must have saved their lives but he got no recognition for it. I did not return home until 4 pm the following day; then my boss rang me at home and instructed me to go back to the pit, to be interviewed by the BBC and ITV for the Six O'Clock News. I refused as I was exhausted after more than thirty-six hours at work.

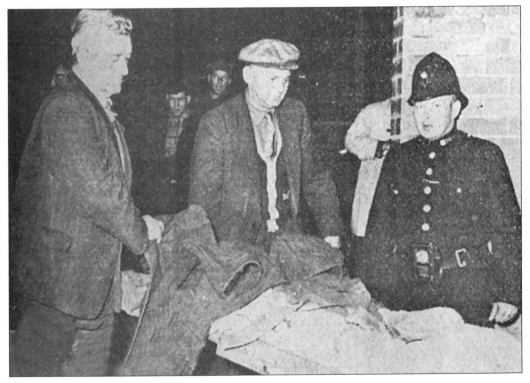

A rescued miner being brought into the medical centre for treatment. Barnsley Chronicle

Albert (or Alfred) Catlin, the first survivor to be brought out of the pit. Barnsley Chronicle

Two miners who escaped from the emission, overman Jack Pattison and Joe Gibbons, had made many attempts to get to the face where the four men died, but without success.

William Sales, chairman of the North Eastern Division of the NCB and Clifford Machin, the Production Director of the Yorkshire Region, arrived at the pit, the latter speaking at an impromtu press conference. He said, at 2.45 am:

> About 7.30 pm Mr Gibbons and Mr Pattison were inspecting the main gate. After both had examined the place, they moved away; Mr Gibbons had got about twenty yards away when he became aware that the main gate was 'on weight'. He turned towards the gate and saw that it was, as he called it, 'Dancing.'
> There were violent vibrations of the roof. he shouted to the men to come out … His oil lamp went out, and he tripped out all the electric switches. There has been a very heavy weight with a large emission of gas, which is slowly clearing.

Casualties at the Rotherham Doncaster Gate Hospital: Leslie France, Luke Brennan, John Hallsworth and Ernest Devine. Sheffield Star

The first man to be rescued alive from the affected area was Alfred Catlin, who was released from the medical centre after a check-up; Morgan Clayton followed, at midnight, now in front of a crowd of 150 watching with great anticipation, including Clayton's wife, who broke down with tears of joy when she saw her husband. Another survivor, Granville Mason, appeared after 1 am, his wife, manageress of the pit canteen, still brewing cups of tea for the rescue workers. Willie Bannister, Allan Martin and Eric Smedley were got out later.

At the inquest it was revealed that a break in the floor resulted in 750,000 cubic feet of gas escaping into the workings.

The men who died were:

Robert Arnott (35), 35 Welland Crescent, Elsecar
Albert Bailey (48), 7 Dearne Road Brampton
John Holmes (46), 15 Cliff Road, Brampton
John Kellett (38), 43 Rufford Avenue, Athersley

Bailey and Holmes, both machinemen, were said to have spent all their working lives at Cortonwood Colliery.

(24) Silverwood

Location: Thrybergh, near Rotherham
Type: Paddy Mail
Fatalities: 10
Date: Thursday, 3 February 1966

Serious underground 'paddy mail' or man-riding accidents, as we have already seen, were rare in South Yorkshire, the previous example being at Sheffield's Nunnery Colliery in 1923 (see entry above). The accident at Silverwood Colliery, on the morning of 3 February 1966, at the start of the day-shift, was a very serious example and, even after almost forty-five years will still be remembered by many former miners, their families and friends.

As mentioned in my introduction to this final section of the book, my intention for the last few entries is to provide an overview of multiple-fatality accidents rather than definitive accounts for which there is insufficient space or indeed complete information; and I remain respectfully conscious of not causing offence to dependants. However, to exclude the last few disasters would result in an incomplete ending for this project. Events at Silverwood, Houghton Main and Bentley, though thankfully infrequent, serve as stark reminders of the dangers of coalmining, even in the modern era; and of course, despite waning statistics and high-profile health and safety, deaths continued into the twenty-first century.

Silverwood Colliery (formerly known as Dalton Main) underwent a considerable amount of capital investment during the 1960s, including the development of the Swallow Wood seam, though both Barnsley and Meltonfield coal were exploited during the interim period. Almost a year after the underground transport disaster, the chairman of the NCB, Lord Robens, visited the colliery since it was now one of only fifty so-called long-life pits in Britain. Further large-scale investment regarding Swallow Wood took place in the mid-

Headline about the Silverwood pit paddy disaster in the Daily Mirror. Daily Mirror

1970s and, following the 1984/85 miners' strike and redundancies, Silverwood continued to operate with very impressive production figures; however, it closed at the end of 1994, plans to develop Parkgate reserves having been abandoned.

A diesel-powered man-riding light locomotive carrying forty day-shift men to their place of work was rammed by an out of control and accelerating supply vehicle. The crash must have been an absolutely horrendous and dreadfully painful experience, with each of the 31 survivors receiving varying injuries; and one, to Jack Nettleship, proving fatal. The resultant shock and psychological impact is incalculable. The rear passenger coach was crushed and many men were trapped in the wreckage. Nine died at the scene.

The next day, Friday, the accident featured in several of national daily newspapers, including *The Times* (p.10) which also included a pit-top image of one of the rescued miners being helped away. *The Times* report appears to have been based on copy obtained from local journalists, referring to one of the survivors (Leslie France, who had been riding in the rear of the carriage) who provided a brief quote, saying: 'I was catapulted out of one carriage into another. I was stunned.' It also mentioned the colliery nursing sister, Diane Adsetts, one of the first medics to reach the scene, who said, 'It was an absolute shambles. the trucks were piled around and men were lying all over the place.' Sister Adsetts went to the assistance of Jack Nettleship who had both of his legs amputated in the crash. The role of 'Sister Diane' was enhanced further in the popular press, perhaps to her own embarrassment, the *Daily Mirror's* account of the accident referring to her as 'the angel of mercy … her face blackened with coal dust and and her pink nail varnish chipped'. However, an 'on duty' first aid man, Jim Bailey, appears to have assisted and treated several of the injured prior to Sister Adsett's arrival. Sisters Kathleen Payne and Mary Parton are also mentioned in the *Mirror* report, as assisting with the injured. Whatever the emphasis, a first-aider, nurses, the more able survivors and the first rescue workers did a tremendous job in doing what they could to help and free the injured. Trainee pit manager John Brown described how jacks and 'anything we could lay our hands on' were used to release trapped men; and another early rescuer was Robert 'Bob' Brocklesby, assisting to remove some of the dead miners, a horrible task.

A narrative and testimonies relating to the accident can be found on John Doxey's excellent website on Silverwood Colliery, dedicated to its miners: http://johndoxey.100 freemb.com/Silverwood/paddytrain.htm

PIT-TRAIN RIDE ENDS IN DEATH

Loco rams miners' coach

BY MIRROR REPORTERS

NINE miners died and thirty-one were injured in a horrifying slow-motion crash half a mile below ground yesterday.

It happened as 50 men were riding a "paddy mail"—the miners' name for an underground train—to the coalface at Silverwood Colliery, near Rotherham, Yorks.

The six-coach paddy slowed down as it approached a junction, and an empty paddy, drawn by a 70 h.p. diesel loco, smashed into it from behind.

The locomotive climbed up the back coach of the packed train, leaping, tearing and twisting ...

Pit safety officer Enoch Hattie scrambled clear of the wreckage and ran to an underground telephone.

His call for help brought rescue teams . . . and the woman who became "The Angel With A Dirty Face," 28-year-old nursing sister Diane Adsetts.

Diane, slightly built and only 5ft. 3in. tall, was down the pit for three hours, caring for the injured.

'Shambles'

When she came up, her face blackened with coal dust and her pink nail varnish chipped, she said wearily:

SISTER DIANE IS 'THE ANGEL OF MERCY'

yesterday's crash were married men with grown-up families.

Men like 51-year-old Jack Coulson, who had five children; 58-year-old Jack Green, father of three; George Smith, 55, another man with five children; Roland Orton, 59, another father of three, and Albert Wraith, 59-year-old father of four.

Telegram

An official investigation began yesterday into the accident, which happened at 8 a.m.

The Prime Minister, Mr. Harold Wilson, sent a telegram to Coal Board chair...

THE RESCUER

Trainee manager John Brown ... "We used

The three 'Angels of Mercy' at Silverwood: Kathleen Payne, Diane Adsetts and Mary Parton. Sheffield Star

The long wait outside Silverwood Colliery. Sheffield Star

A helping hand at Silverwood for an injured workmate. Sheffield Star

As one would expect there was extensive coverage in the Saturday editions of local and regional newspapers, including the *South Yorkshire Times* of 5 February, who reported that John A Brown (27) was one of the first on the scene after the accident, describing him as an engineering trainee. Nursing Sister Kathleen Payne had driven from Denaby Colliery as soon as she had heard the news, saying, 'When I got to the scene there were bodies laid out waiting to be moved … I helped lift them out of the pit'. Nurse Mary Parton summed up the effort: 'I don't know how many miles we walked but we are all absolutely exhausted.'

At the inquest in Rotherham, presided over by Coroner Dr HH Pilling, identification and the causes of death of the miners were confirmed. Most were recorded as 'multiple injuries' but there several who died due to a combination of shock, respiratory and cardiac failure.

The main recommendation of the official inquiry was that a train conveying materials should not be allowed to follow a passenger-carrying train. The rules for the operation of underground man-riding operations were re-written accordingly.

According to *Hansard*, the Silverwood Colliery accident was discussed in parliament on the day it took place, 3 February 1966. The Minister of Power, Fred Lee MP, read a brief statement (in response to David Griffiths MP), saying that investigations were proceeding and he was awaiting a further report from HM Divisional Inspector of Mines. The mood of the House was ably portrayed by Griffiths (Member for Rother Valley), who responded with the following:

This is another example of the price which has to be paid for coal. It should be thoroughly understood Members on both sides that, regardless of the safety precautions which are put on the Statute Book that this is the most dangerous and arduous occupation in the whole world.

Earlier, the Labour Prime Minister, Harold Wilson, sent the following telegram to Lord Robens, Chairman of the NCB:

> I was greatly distressed to learn of the accident at Silverwood this morning, and of the casualties suffered. Will you please send my deepest sympathy to the bereaved families and to those who were injured.

According to the *Colliery Guardian* (June 1975), a further underground train crash occurred at Silverwood on 16 May 1975 when one man was injured and five others were slightly hurt. A royal visit to Silverwood, by HM Queen and Prince Philip, a few weeks later, on 30 July 1975, took place in far happier circumstances to the one experienced by their forbears, in 1912, after the Cadeby tragedy.

The men who died were:

Jack W Coulson (51), salvage worker, 143 Oaks Lane, Kimberworth Park
Jack Green (50, 58 in one report), salvage worker, 2 March Bank, Thrybergh
J Hanton (59), 6 Park Grove, Bramley
Reginald Kelsall (60), back ripper, 10 Silver Street, Thrybergh
Jack Nettleship* (53), Sandy Drive, Ravenfield
Roland 'Roly' H Orton (49, 59 in one report), back ripper, 30 Oldfield Road, East Herringthorpe
James B Sansome (61), salvage worker, 49 Osberton Street, Dalton
Arthur Shaw (51), back ripper, 33 Lincoln Street, Maltby
George Smith (55) chock maintenance man, Pear Tree Avenue, Bramley
A Wraith (59), back ripper, 23 Broadway East, East Dene

*Jack died three days after the accident

(25) Houghton Main

Location: Little Houghton, Wombwell, Barnsley
Type: Explosion
Fatalities: 5
Date: Thursday, 12 June 1975

On what was said to be the warmest night of the year, at about 6.50 pm, during the sixth day of a heatwave, an explosion in the depths of Houghton Main Colliery resulted in the deaths of five men. The accident took place only two years after an inrush of water from old workings killed seven miners at Lofthouse Colliery, near Wakefield, in West Yorkshire, sixteen miles away. In the same year as the flooding, 1973, eighteen men died in a terrible pit cage disaster at Markham Main, near Chesterfield and five miners died when a roof collapsed at Seaforth Colliery, Kirkcaldy, in Scotland.

Houghton Main employed 1,361 men (1191 underground) and was linked to Grimethorpe Colliery where the combined coal production was wound to the surface. Development relating to the 6ft 6in Newhill seam was nearing completion, expected to be worked as from 16 June, to replace B 04s face in the 4ft 2in Meltonfield seam which lay 98 feet below.

Anxious women wait for news, a picture evocative of Victorian disasters. Sheffield Star

The Houghton event stunned local communities, was a stark reminder of the dangers still inherent in mining coal and attracted widespread media attention. At the scene and during the subsequent debate and inquiry, the new Yorkshire miners' leader Arthur Scargill (elected President of the Yorkshire Area NUM in 1973), had taken over the charismatic advocacy of predecessors, such as Herbert Smith and Joe Hall.

Most of the daily newspapers reported the event on the front pages of their Friday editions; as usual the tabloids using sensationalist headlines. Initially, only two deaths were known (from a small group of six men) and rescue teams and volunteers worked through the night to reach the other men, although handicapped by a roof fall. THREE TRAPPED IN DEATH PIT was the headline in the *Daily Mirror* whose report included an early quote from Arthur Scargill, who said: 'It is bad. There must have been a violent explosion.' A local pit inspector, Peter Barney, was also quoted as saying: 'This is the real price of coal – men getting killed and the hours of anxiety.' The NCB Barnsley Area director, John Keirs, explained that the men were working with an electric motor at the time of the explosion, on a 'risk' job. They were part of a development team, one of the most dangerous of all underground operations. The staff reporter at the *Daily Express* focused on the rescue operations, under the emotive headline: BATTLE IN PIT TOMB, but included more detailed quotes. Arthur Scargill, about to go underground himself, said: 'Our fear now is that there might be a second blast. We don't know what caused the first and another one can happen. The whole district is filled with carbon monoxide … no one can go near without breathing apparatus.' Scargill also explained that there was hope that the missing men were in an air

The Daily Mirror *featured the Houghton Main accident on it's front page.* Daily Mirror

pocket and that the first rescue team had used up their oxygen supply searching for the men, therefore had to return to their fresh air base. A second team had taken over at midnight. The first team had brought out the bodies of the two dead men (Richard Bannister and Raymond Copperwheat). A faceworker, Ken Upperdine, aged 38, was recovered alive. Upperdine had, perhaps fortuitously, moved some distance away from his colleagues that died in or near the Meltonfield seam, in order to make a phone call. Nevertheless, the blast knocked him off his feet and he sustained serious facial burns and other injuries. He had only returned to work a few days earlier following injuries received in other accidents at the pit.

The Houghton Main explosion was also featured on national and regional radio and television; and of course in considerable detail, over several months, in the *Barnsley Chronicle*.

Early visitors to the pit on the Friday included the Labour politician, Tony Benn, Secretary of State for Energy and Sir Derek Ezra, chairman of the NCB. On the same day, in Parliament, the Bolsover MP Dennis Skinner said that any investigation should examine whether further safeguards were needed. The Minister of State (Employment), Albert Booth, supported Mr Skinner's comments, paying tribute to the rescue teams. Booth stated that

Front-page headlines in the Daily Express.
Daily Express

DAILY EXP

No. 23,317   Friday June 13 1975   Weather: Dry, sunny

Race for life after two die 1,000 ft. down

BATTLE IN PIT TOMB

Express Staff Reporter Harry Cooke

EARLY this morning rescue teams were battling to reach three men missing 1,000ft. underground after a mystery explosion ripped through a pit, killing two and injuring another.

Distraught relatives huddled at the pit gates of Houghton Main Colliery, near Barnsley, Yorkshire, amid the glare of rescue workers' lamps.

But no one knew

Rescuers and volunteers at Houghton Main. Barnsley Chronicle

the accident would be investigated by the inspectors of mines, with the co-operation of the NCB and NUM.

Benn's comments were highlighted in the *Barnsley Chronicle*'s report, published on 20 June: 'This tragedy may remind people, as it has reminded me, that there is still a very high price to be paid in human life for the coal we get in this country.'

Dr Herbert Pilling, the South Yorkshire district coroner, warned against 'theories' and 'rumours' about the cause of the disaster when the inquest was opened on Tuesday, 17 June, principally for formal identification of the deceased miners.

The Newhall seam and equipment, said to be worth £750,000 (almost £8 million today), was sealed off by the time the inquest had started, as was part of the Meltonfield. This was due to high readings of carbon monoxide, suggesting 'heatings' or fires in the affected workings, which would be closed for safety reasons for at least nine months. This stopped any further search for evidence at the seat of the explosion.

In the meantime, on behalf of the miners' union, Scargill continued to press for an official inquiry. Speaking at the NUM annual conference in July, during a bitter debate at the time of the government's social contract policy, he said: 'No one can say that mineworkers are not worth £100 (c. £1,000 today) a week in 1975,' in the context of the recent pit disasters; and now rather than later.

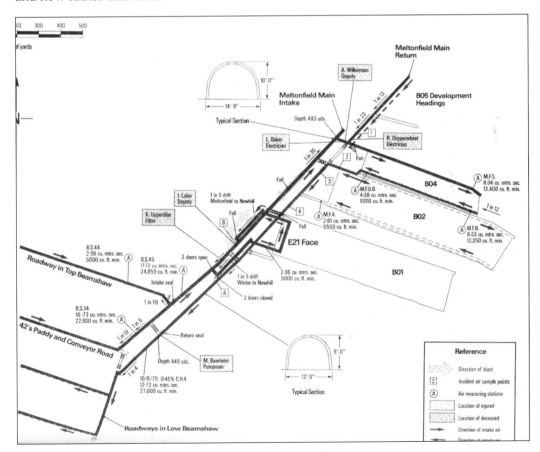

Detail from a plan showing the accident scene. Author's collection

An inquiry was instigated, opening in the Council Chamber of the Town Hall, Barnsley, on 26 August and lasted for nine days, during which 81 persons gave evidence, under the direction of Mr J Carver, HM Chief Inspector of Mines and reported to Mr W Simpson, chairman of the Health and Safety Commission. The final submissions, heard on 4 September, included one from Arthur Scargill on behalf of the Yorkshire NUM, in which he urged action over breaches of rules before the disaster, particularly in respect of a faulty fan and an unventilated heading.

The Inquiry report was published on 18 November 1975. Carver concluded that the explosion 'resulted from the ignition of an accumulation of firedamp in B 05s return development heading which had been unventilated for a period of nine days prior to the explosion'. He also stated that the most likely source of ignition was 'frictional sparking' from the impeller and casing of the Carter Howden auxiliary fan.

The men who died were:

Leonard Baker (53), electrician, Charles Street, Little Houghton
Richard Bannister (31), pumpman, Coronation Avenue, Grimethorpe
Raymond Copperwheat (42), electrician, Neville Crescent, Darfield
Irvin Lakin (55), deputy, Wath Road, Wombwell
Frederick Arnold Williamson (59), deputy, Norfolk Road, Great Houghton

Although the disaster and its aftermath attracted many experts and well-known people, there is no doubt that the heroes of the day were the almost anonymous volunteers and rescue team members; and, of course, we must not forgot the feelings of the hundreds of miners and their families who were affected in various ways, some temporarily and others no doubt for the rest of their lives, by the sad event of the summer of 1975. I've met and talked to several Houghton miners over the years but one of the most compelling testimonies that I have come across was written by Alec Wilkinson. Leaving home at 8.45 pm, Alec arrived at the pit expecting to work on the night shift but found himself, along with his younger brother and close colleagues, as one of sixteen volunteers assisting the rescue team:

As we walked across the pit yard, to the No 1 shaft, cap lamps and respirators already being collected, we saw one of the missing men, fitter Ken Upperdine, had been brought to the surface … His face and hands were very badly burned and he was suffering from numerous broken bones. Ken's family had lived next door to my own all through my childhood … When we did arrive we were told we would be needed for stretcher bearing …

The rescue teams, who were already down the pit, had established a fresh-air base, where it was safe for us to proceed to without breathing apparatus. As we travelled inbye from the pit bottom we could not help but notice the thick black dust, which had settled over the full length of the paddy road, and we told ourselves that no-one could have possibly survived, what undoubtedly would have been a living nightmare; but then Ken Upperdine was still alive, so hope was not gone.

No sooner though, had we arrived at the fresh-air base, when we were struck by the full force of the most horrifying experience of our lives, a dead workmate. At first we did not know who it was, as he lay covered up by a dark blanket and strapped to a stretcher…Six of us were then detailed by the doctor to take the dead man out of the pit. As we were waiting for the paddy … we were informed that the motionless body underneath the blankets was that of Dick Bannister. Dick was one of the nicest men a person could have wished to know; a handsome, strapping young man, who would go out his way to help anyone … found ten yards the wrong side of a set of air doors …probably ten yards from safety, ten bloody yards … When we reached the surface we lifted our dead workmate into a waiting ambulance, while at the same time being blinded by television camera lights and the flashing of photographers' bulbs.

Alec then described, on returning underground, how he came across his younger brother and five others, carrying the body of Irvin Lakin out of the pit, '… a God-fearing man, who always carried a small Bible down the mine with him … the tattered pages of his once-proud possession were still to be found, rustling in the air which had turned foul on him'. The retrieval of the body of colliery electrician Raymond Copperwheat 'who had only the previous week done some work for one of my elder brothers' was then recounted, along with news that Len Baker and Arni Williamson had been found dead. 'Very few words were spoken on our return journey to the colliery surface, it had all been said,' Alec concluded.

Local author Barry Hines' play *The Price of Coal* (Part Two), televised in 1977 (published in book form two years later), and directed by Ken Loach, appeared in the wake of the Lofthouse and Houghton Main pit disasters.

(26) Bentley Colliery

Location: Bentley, Doncaster
Type: Paddy mail
Fatalities: 7
Date: Tuesday, 21 November 1978

Although serious accidents in coal mines, particularly explosions, were becoming far less common, the Bentley man-riding disaster highlighted a disturbing factor already apparent in district inspectors' reports: accidents due to underground transport were bucking the trend. The Silverwood paddy mail crash of 1966 was relatively fresh in the memory of South Yorkshire's miners and, a few days after the Bentley tragedy, an underground man-riding train at Elsecar Colliery was derailed, luckily without anyone suffering serious injury.

The accident occurred within a few hours of the 47th anniversary of the Bentley disaster of 20 November 1931 (see above).

Diesel-powered locomotives had been introduced underground at Bentley in 1939, principally for man-riding, but extended to coal haulage in 1945. They were used for conveying both men and coal until 1968, when trunk conveyor belts were introduced for the latter. By 1978, a fleet of twelve locos were used, varying in age from 22–33 years, made by Hunslet Limited. The maximum speed was 9.15 mph (in 2nd gear). The seven which had mechanical brakes were generally used exclusively for materials. The five other locos had both air and mechanical brakes so were used for man-riding and materials. A diesel garage near the pit bottom was the control and service point underground. The man-riding trains were equipped with radios for the driver to communicate with the controller. The passenger trains consisted of a locomotive and four coupled carriages, each divided into

Bentley Colliery. Author's collection

four compartments which could carry six men, though a local agreement specified no more than five. Thus there was a maximum capacity of twenty men per carriage.

Up to the time of the accident regional courses were run at Bentley for trainee loco drivers.

At 4.45 am, sixty-five men were returning to the shaft bottom at the end of their night shift, when the man-riding train in which they were travelling ran out of control down a 1 in 16 incline. The paddy was derailed after failing to negotiate a curve at the foot of the incline, crashing into the steel arched roadway support, in a tunnel 12 ft high and 14ft wide. A track-mounted arrestor device did not stop the runaway vehicle as it had done in an incident only two weeks earlier. The arrestor's impact head had been deliberately fixed in the lowered position, so could not function. A red warning light indicating this malfunction had been showing for several weeks.

The course of the accident was compounded by the employment of an untrained conductor (driver's assistant), who sat in the carriage that did not form part of the passenger train and therefore was not in a position to apply the emergency brakes. This man was placed on duty in error, having no proper training or qualifications. The driver himself only had twenty-three days' driving experience, and had only been trained for skid procedures in a locomotive of different characteristics and controls.

A further breach of regulations became apparent when the track gradient, routinely tested three months earlier, showed that eight pairs of rails exceeded the 1 in 15 limit, but no remedial action was taken.

The colliery rescue team arrived quickly and within two hours the dead and injured were brought to the surface. Among the first external people at the scene were Arthur Scargill, president of the Yorkshire Area NUM, his colleagues, Owen Briscoe and R Horbury and members of the Bentley NUM Branch committee; also soon present were three inspectors, managers and Jack Wood, the NCB's Doncaster Area director. Later arrivals included Derek Ezra, the NCB chairman, Joe Gormley, NUM president and Tony Benn, the Secretary of State for Energy, who visited the injured in hospital.

The report from the Yorkshire Area NUM praised the rescue operation:

> After the accident the workmen, management and officials joined forces in an exemplary manner and applied themselves unflinchingly to the task of recovering and releasing the dead and injured.

The coroner for Doncaster, Mr K Potter, opened the inquest, principally for identification of the deceased, on 24 November, prior to the usual adjournment in order to compile information and plan a schedule of evidence.

The official investigation and report on the causes and circumstances attending the locomotive man-riding accident at Bentley Colliery, on 21 November 1978, was carried out by the South Yorkshire District of HM Inspectorate of Mines and Quarries, with assistance of Headquarters staff. It was published remarkably quickly, at a press conference in Doncaster, on 3 October 1978.

A modern man-riding train, this example from a French coal mine. Author's collection

The report concluded that the accident occurred by the train running away on the incline and getting out of control, before crashing into roadway supports at the D04/D05 junction.

It stated that the engagement of second gear by the driver meant that he was unable to stop or control the speed of the train and that this was against the Manager's Transport Rules. Furthermore, had the brakes been properly applied, the train would have been brought to rest. It was also noted that the guard was not in a position to operate the emergency brake valve as he was not sitting in a carriage that formed part of the passenger train.

The report also confirmed that the track was inclined at too steep a gradient, contrary to regulation; and that the Godwin Warren arrestor had been 'deliberately defeated', so could not stop the runaway.

Eleven separate recommendations were made, including 'strict discipline and adherence to the Manager's Transport Rules', the certification and authorisation of locomotive drivers, who should be given a reasonable period of post-qualification experience before being permitted to drive man-riding trains. The report was to be submitted to various committees which had been established at National and Area level to study the problem of safety in regard to underground locomotive transport.

Those who died were:

Robert Aitcheson (54), faceworker
Donald Box (39), faceworker
Kenneth Green (38), faceworker
David R Hall (21), face trainee
Geoffrey Henderson (39), faceworker
Michael Edward Hickman (18), face trainee
James Mitchell (55), face worker

Those seriously injured were:

J Butcher (57), shift charge engineer
Thomas J Rush (26), supply man
Paul Thompson (26), ripper

Only two years afterwards, on 10 December 1979, three men were killed in another paddy mail accident, at Kinsley Drift, in West Yorkshire.

Glossary of Mining Terms

afterdamp	a mixture of non-inflamable gases left following an explosion. Dangerous and deadly, often killing more miners than the explosion.
agent	a director of a colliery company, usually with knowledge and expertise in the coal mining industry.
banksman	person in charge of the surface/pit-top who controlled access of men/materials into the cage, collect tallies/checks and signal the winding engineman to indicate that it was safe to descend.
box-hole	underground cabin sited near the pit bottom, an office.
cage	a timber or metal compartment/lift, single, double or triple-decked, into which men or materials are transported up and down a shaft. Also known as a chair.
chock	a short prop or roof support of timber or steel (the latter usually hydraulically operated).
corporal	a chargehand, responsible for a group of men.
coal-cutter	a machine for extracting coal, usually electronically driven.
coalface	solid area where coal is extracted manually or by machinery.
contractor	a miner employed at an agreed rate of pay, usually for a set period.
crossgate	junction/area between underground roadways.
dataller	a day-wage, general duty miner.
deputy	a qualified official in charge of a district, whose responsibilities includes the overseeing of safety in the context of coalmining legislation.
district	an underground area of the mine where coal is extracted, usually with a geographic name and/or number.
downcast	a shaft through which fresh air enters the mine. Usually numbered.
dudley	a round metal container in which drinking water is kept and carried. Various capacities.
engineman	a person employed to operate a winding engine at the surface or undergound.
filler	a miner whose chief job is to load coal into tubs or on to a conveyor belt.
firedamp	inflammable gas (in certain quantities eg 5–15% highly dangerous), chiefly methane, released from coal seams and old workings, the origin of explosions. It accumulates in roof cavities if ventilation is inadequate. Colourless, tasteless, odourless and invisible to the eye.
fitter	a qualified person who maintains, repairs and helps install mining machinery and equipment above and below ground.
flagsheet	also known as a flatsheet, a metal sheet attached to the bottom of a cage from a landing area so as to assist the exit and entrance of miners.
goaf	also known as a 'gob', a waste, abandoned area of old workings.
gob	see goaf.
hanger-on	a miner with responsibility for placing flagsheets to cages and signaling to the winding engineman.
heading	a drivage in advance of any coalface, to determine conditions ahead.

inbye	a term to describe the relative position of anyone in the mine eg 'he has gone inbye' or towards the face. cf outbye.
level	a horizontal drivage tunnel which follows the seam of coal from the face. Can be at an angle.
longwall	a system of mining coal with all the colliers in a district manning one long coal-face, either hand-got or machine-got.
Main	in Yorkshire, used in colliery names where the principal seam was originally the Barnsley bed eg Wath Main Colliery.
maingate	the main underground roadway of a mine; also known as 'mother gate'.
NCB	National Coal Board.
NUM	National Union of Mineworkers.
official	generic term for all levels of management from an agent to a shot-firer.
onsetter	equivalent of the banksman but in the pit bottom, in charge of access into and out of the cage; operates signals heard by the winder and banksman at the surface.
outbye	a term used to denote the relative position of anyone in a mine eg he has gone outbye ie away from the face towards the pit bottom. cf inbye
overman	a senior official of immediate higher rank than a deputy, responsible for a wider area that a deputy.
pack/packer	a stacked roof support made of stone, similar to a drystone wall; a person building a pack.
paddy mail	underground man-riding vehicle either rope or diesel driven that carried miners towards their place of work.
pan/panman	part of a panzer stage loader through which the chain was guided; many pans were coupled together/workman with responsibility for maintaining, turning etc the pans.
pillar and stall	a system of mining a seam by extracting the coal in parallel stalls advancing onwards. Cross-cuts were driven at right-angles every 25 yards to link up to the stalls, leaving pillars of coal to support the roof.
Price List	a booklet containing agreed rates of pay at a particular colliery.
return gate	see tailgate.
ripper	workman who removes rock above a coal seam/heading and sets supporting steel rings/arches.
shot-firer	a qualified person who fires shots of explosives in a district.
skip	a large container in which coal is raised up the shaft.
stint	an allocated distance along a coalface where a miner works during his shift.
stone dust	crushed limestone, spread along roadways to reduce the impact of a coal dust explosion.
stoppings	airtight barriers erected with sandbags etc in order to seal off dangerous or disused working areas.
tailgate	an underground roadway leading to the end of a longwall face; also known as the return or supply gate.
trammer	a young miner (usually) who pushes full and empty tubs or trams of coal along rail lines.
upcast	a shaft through which stale air returns to the surface. Usually numbered.
YMA	Yorkshire Miners Association.

Sources and Bibliography

Eyewitness/Family History
Reg Batterham (Barnsley Main, 1942)
Walter Caswell (Wharncliffe Woodmoor, 1936)
Barry Crabtree (Cadeby 1912 & Cortonwood 1961)
Sidney Cutts (Manvers Main, 1945)
Arthur Daniels (Maltby, 1923)
Fred Elliott (Wharncliffe Woodmoor, 1936)
Jack Faulkner (Barnsley Main, 1947)
Andy Featherstone (Aldwarke, 1904)
Mrs Enid Green (Barnsley Main, 1942)
Lynn Haines (Aldwarke, 1904)
Tommy Henwood (Bentley, 1931)
Peter Humphries (Cadeby, 1912)
George Kemp (Wharncliffe Woodmoor, 1936)
Doris Kitching (Bentley, 1931)
Ted Lunness (Barnburgh, 1942 & Cortonwood 1961)
Lord Mason of Barnsley (Wharncliffe Woodmoor, 1936)
Sam Owens (Wharncliffe Woodmoor, 1936)
Ron Palmer (Wharncliffe Woodmoor, 1936)
Jack Parkin (Wharncliffe Woodmoor, 1936)
Mrs D Smith (Bentley, 1931)
Edward Thompson (Cadeby, 1912)
Alec Wilkinson (Houghton Main, 1975)

Primary Printed
Clayton, Arthur K, *Hoyland Nether*, Author's collection, n.d (1973)
Explosion at Cortonwood Colliery 1932, People & Mining Publication, n.d.
Hopkinson, Keith, *The Story of the Hoyland Silkstone Colliery and the Winning of the First Edward Medal for Bravery*, 2000, unpublished MS (Barnsley Local Studies & Archives).
Thompson, Edward, notes about his boyhood (courtesy of Karen Walker & Francis Thompson)

Books
Arnot, R Page, *The Miners: One Union*, One Industry, George Allen & Unwin, London, 1979
Arnot, R Page, *The Miners: Years of Struggle*, George Allen & Unwin, 1953
Arnot, R Page, *The Miners in Crisis and War*, George Allen & Unwin Ltd, London, 1961
Auckland, Rev Clifford, *The Growth of a Township. Maltby's Story*, Rotherham MBC Libraries, Museum and Arts Department, 1989
Bailey, Catherine, *Black Diamonds. The Rise and Fall of a Dynasty*, Viking (Penguin), 2007
Baylies, Carolyn, *The History of the Yorkshire Miners 1881–1918*, Routledge, 1993

Dictionary of National Biography

Dodsworth, Anthony, *Around Rawmarsh and Parkgate*, Tempus Publishing Ltd, Stroud, 2002

Duncan, Lily, *Collier Lad*, Write Books, 2005

Elliott, Brian (ed), *Aspects of Doncaster*, Wharncliffe Publishing Ltd, 1997

Elliott, Brian, *Pits & Pitmen of Barnsley*, Wharncliffe Books, Barnsley, 2001

Elliott, Brian, *Lord Mason. Barnsley. Pitlad to Peer*, Wharncliffe Books, 2008

Elliott, Brian, *Royston, Carlton & Monk Bretton*, Sutton, Stroud, 2000

Elliott, Brian, *South Yorkshire Mining Disasters*, Vol 1, The Nineteenth Century, Wharncliffe Books, Barnsley 2006

Elliott, Brian, *Yorkshire Mining Veterans*, Wharncliffe Books, 2005

Ellis, Norman, *South Yorkshire Collieries on old picture postcards*, Reflections of a Bygone Age, 1995

Fleming, Alex and Hird, Stephen, *Wath-upon-Dearne As It Was*, Hendon Publishing Company Limited, 1982

Goodchild, John, *South Yorkshire Collieries*, Tempus Publishing Ltd, Stroud, 2001

Goodman, John, *Sheffield in the Seventies*, Breedon Books, Derby, 2002

Goodman, Peter, *Sheffield in the Sixties*, Breedon Books, Derby, 2001

Greathead, June & Tony, *Photographs of Old Conisbrough*, self-published,1990

Henderson, DV, *Heroic Endeavour*, JB Hayward, 1988

Hill, Alan, *The South Yorkshire Coalfield. A History and Development*, Tempus Publishing Ltd, Stroud, 2001

Jones, Karen & John Lloyd, *A Portrait of My Father*, Upfront Publishing, Peterborough, 2008.

MacFarlane, J E, *The Blood on Your Coal*, Doncaster Library Service, nd (1985)

Mason, Roy, *Paying the Price*, Robert Hale, London, 1999

Neville, Robert G, *The Yorkshire Miners in Camera*, Hendon Publishing Co Ltd, Nelson (Lancs), 1976

Orwell, George, *The Road to Wigan Pier*, Penguin Books Ltd, Harmondsworth, 1962

Redmayne, Sir Richard A S, *Men, Mines and Memories*, Eyre & Spottiswoode Ltd, London, 1942

Sampson, Michael, *Kiveton Park Colliery 1866–1994*, Kiveton Park & Wales History Society, Kiveton, 2007

Threlkeld, John, *Pits*, Wharncliffe Publishing Ltd, Barnsley, 1987

Threlkeld, John, *Pits 2*, Wharncliffe Publushing Ltd, Barnsley, 1989

Vernon, Frank, *The Day the Earth Trembled*, Doncaster Library Service, Doncaster, 1989

Wilson, Reverend Jesse, *The Story of the Great Struggle, 1902–03*, Christian Commonwealth Co Ltd, 1904

Who Was Who, Oxford University Press

Wilson, WH et al, *The Order of Industrial Heroism,* The Orders and Medals Research Society, 2000

Woodhead, John, *The Bentley Pit Disaster*, Waterdale Press (Doncaster Library and Information Services), 1991

Newspapers/Magazines

Barnsley Chronicle and South Yorkshire News
Colliery Guardian
Daily Express

Daily Mirror
Daily Sketch
Doncaster Chronicle
Doncaster Gazette
Leeds Mercury
Maltby News
Manchester Guardian
Memories of Barnsley
Mexborough & Swinton Times
New York Times
Rotherham Advertiser
Sheffield Daily Telegraph
Sheffield Star
South Kirkby, South Elmsall & Hemsworth Times
South Yorkshire Times
South Yorkshire Times & Express
The Times
Yorkshire Evening News
Yorkshire Post

Official reports

HM Mines Inspectors' Reports (annual)

HM MInes Inspectors' Reports, specific:

Explosions at Barnsley Main Colliery, Yorkshire. Report on the causes of, and circumstances attending the explosions etc on 16 and 17 February 1942 by JR Felton OBE, HM Deputy Inspector of Mines.

Report on the causes and circumstances attending the explosion, which occurred at Barnsley Main Colliery, Yorkshire, on the 7th May 1947 by HJ Humphrys DSO, MBE, HM Divisional Inspector of Mines.

Report on the causes and circumstances attending the explosion, which occurred in the North East District, Barnsley seam, at the Bentley Colliery, Doncaster, Yorkshire, on the 20th November 1931, by Sir Henry Walker, HM Chief Inspector of Mines.

Report on the causes and circumstances attending the locomotive manriding accident, which occurred at Bentley Colliery, South Yorkshire, on 21 November 1978, by HM Inspectorate of Mines and Quarries.

Report on the causes and circumstances attending the explosions, which occurred at the Cadeby Main Colliery, on Tuesday, July 9th, 1912, by Sir Richard Redmayne, HM Chief Inspector of Mines.

Report on causes and circumstances attending the explosion at Houghton Main Colliery, South Yorkshire on 12 June 1975, by Mr J Carver, HM Chief Inspector of Mines (reporting to Mr W Simpson, Chairman of the Health & Safety Commission.

Report on the causes and circumstances attending the explosion, which occurred on 4th March, 1945, at Manvers Main Colliery, Wath-on-Dearne, Yorkshire, by J.R. Felton, OBE, HM Chief Inspector of Mines.

Report on the causes and circumstances attending the explosion, which occurred at Maltby Main Colliery, Yorkshire, on 28 July 1923, by Sir Thomas Mottram, CBE, HM Chief Inspector of Mines.

Report on the causes and circumstances attending the explosion at North Gawber (Lidgett) Colliery, Yorkshire, on 12th September, 1935, by Sir Henry Walker CBE, HM Chief Inspector of Mines.

Report on the causes and circumstances attending the underground haulage accident at the Nunnery Colliery, near Sheffield, on the 3rd December 1923, by Sir Thomas Mottram, CBE, formerly HM Chief Inspector of Mines.

Report on the causes and circumstances attending the explosion, which occurred at the Wharncliffe Silkstone Colliery, on the 30th May 1914, by Samuel Pope, Barrister at Law and Thomas H Mottram one of HM Inspectors of Mines.

Report into the causes and circumstances attending the shaft accident, which occurred at the No 2 shaft at Thorne Colliery, Thorne, Yorkshire, on 15 March 1926 by Major H.M. Hudspeth, D.S.O., M.C., M.Sc., Divisional Inspector of Mines.

Report on the causes and circumstances attending the explosion, which occurred at Wharncliffe Woodmoor Nos 1, 2 and 3 Colliery, Yorkshire, on 6 August 1936, by Sir Henry Walker CBE, HM Chief Inspector of Mines.

Report on the causes and circumstances attending the explosion, which occurred at Wath Main Colliery, Wath-upon-Dearne, Yorkshire, on the 24th February 1930, by Sir Henry Walker CBE, HM Chief Inspector of Mines.

Hansard (various editions)

Articles

Rose Johnson, 'George Orwell and the Road to Pogmoor Sands', in Brian Elliott (ed), *Aspects of Barnsley 5*, 1998

Brian Elliott, 'Disaster at Wharncliffe Woodmoor', in *Memories of Barnsley*, Autumn, 2009

Digital/internet

Wikipedia

University of Glasgow Archive Services (John Brown & Company)

http://www.rotherhamweb.co.uk/cadeby

http://www.dmm.org.uk (Durham Mining Museum)

www..cmhrc.co.uk (Coalmining History Resource Centre/Raleys)

http://www.heroesofminesrescue.co.uk (Philip Clifford)

Index